THE FUTURE OF THE NORTH AMERICAN FREE TRADE AGREEMENT

HEARING

BEFORE THE

SUBCOMMITTEE ON TERRORISM, NONPROLIFERATION, AND TRADE

OF THE

COMMITTEE ON FOREIGN AFFAIRS
HOUSE OF REPRESENTATIVES

ONE HUNDRED FIFTEENTH CONGRESS

FIRST SESSION

DECEMBER 12, 2017

Serial No. 115–90

Printed for the use of the Committee on Foreign Affairs

Available via the World Wide Web: http://www.foreignaffairs.house.gov/ or
http://www.gpo.gov/fdsys/

U.S. GOVERNMENT PUBLISHING OFFICE

27–810PDF   WASHINGTON : 2018

CONTENTS

Page

WITNESSES

Mr. Eric Farnsworth, vice president, Council of the Americas 8
Mr. Daniel Allford, president, ARC Specialties 17
The Honorable John D. Negroponte, vice chairman, McLarty Associates (former Deputy Secretary of State and Former Director of National Intelligence) 23
Ms. Celeste Drake, Trade and Globalization Policy specialist, The American Federation of Labor and Congress of Industrial Organizations 29

LETTERS, STATEMENTS, ETC., SUBMITTED FOR THE HEARING

The Honorable Ted Poe, a Representative in Congress from the State of Texas, and chairman, Subcommittee on Terrorism, Nonproliferation, and Trade: Prepared statement 4
Mr. Eric Farnsworth: Prepared statement 11
Mr. Daniel Allford: Prepared statement 19
The Honorable John D. Negroponte: Prepared statement 25
Ms. Celeste Drake: Prepared statement 31

APPENDIX

Hearing notice 58
Hearing minutes 59
The Honorable Darrell E. Issa, a Representative in Congress from the State of California:
Prepared statement 60
Material submitted for the record 61

THE FUTURE OF THE NORTH AMERICAN FREE TRADE AGREEMENT

TUESDAY, DECEMBER 12, 2017

House of Representatives,
Subcommittee on Terrorism, Nonproliferation, and Trade,
Committee on Foreign Affairs,
Washington, DC.

The subcommittee met, pursuant to notice, at 2:00 p.m., in room 2172, Rayburn House Office Building, Hon. Ted Poe (chairman of the subcommittee) presiding.

Mr. POE. The subcommittee will come to order.

Without objection, all members may have 5 days to submit statements, questions, extraneous materials for the record, subject to the length limitation in the rules.

I will now make my opening statement.

Twenty-three years ago, the North American Free Trade Agreement revolutionized trade and investment between the U.S., Canada, and Mexico. We share thousands of miles of border with Canada and Mexico. They are our neighbors and our natural partners in trade and security.

And I want to emphasize the word "neighbors." Sometimes the United States seems to be more concerned about some country far, far away than they are about our neighbors, Mexico and Canada. I think that is a mistake.

This partnership has been shaped by NAFTA and our mutual histories. I am a strong supporter of free trade. America's strength is closely connected to its economic well-being. When we break down trade barriers, American trade and American jobs increase.

Trade is the lifeblood of my home State of Texas. Last year in Texas, almost 1 million jobs were supported by some form of trade. Texas has been the top exporting State in the United States for 14 consecutive years. The overwhelming majority of Texas exporters are not big corporations but 93 percent of the Texas exporters are small and medium-size businesses.

In my district of Houston, over half of the economy depends on trade. Houston has one of the largest ports in the world and is the oil and gas capital of the world. And guess where our Texas exporters export the most? Mexico and Canada, our NAFTA partners. Mexico is Texas' number-one exporting partner. Over 10,000 trucks a day pass the Texas-Mexico border, all involved in trade.

Texas is just one of the many States that rely on NAFTA to fuel the economy. Study after study have shown that increased trade leads to increased jobs for all Americans. More jobs mean more wealth for Americans. NAFTA supports 14 million jobs in the United States, and, thanks to NAFTA, trade between the U.S., Mexico, and Canada has tripled. Nearly every industry is affected in one way or another by NAFTA. The U.S. economy relies on NAFTA.

Free trade agreements like NAFTA do more than just grow our economy. Trade is one of our best tools for foreign policy and political policy. We have seen the connection between free trade and freedom, opportunity, and prosperity. When we signed the NAFTA agreement, Mexico was considered a developing country. Its economy was one of the most closed in the world. Now, thanks in part to NAFTA, Mexico has an open economy valued at $2.2 trillion. The growth has made Mexico a stable neighbor.

The increased trade between our countries has also deepened the ties between Mexico and Canada, allowing us to work together on many critical issues. Today, we cooperate with the Mexican Government on numerous issues, surprisingly to some Americans, including border security, immigration, and the fight against organized crime and drug trafficking. Our southern border security depends on our joint effort with Mexico.

Cooperation with Canada has improved due to NAFTA. Our forces train and work together to defend North America. We fight side-by-side against national security threats like ISIS, and we are NATO partners. These are some of the most critical issues to our national security and to the security of our world.

That brings me to the reason we are having this hearing today, to address the renegotiation of this critical free trade agreement. This negotiation, or renegotiation, is going on as we speak.

A lot has changed in 23 years. The internet has transformed the way companies do business. Reforms in Mexico have created new opportunities for U.S. businesses. The renegotiation presents an opportunity to update the agreement in areas like energy, e-commerce, customs and trade facilitation, and many others to strengthen and promote trade.

While there is a lot of opportunity to strengthen the agreement, there is also the risk of hurting U.S. businesses and workers. Hundreds of thousands of jobs across North America could be at risk if we suddenly pulled out of NAFTA or weakened the agreement. We could also do damage to our partnerships with Mexico and Canada that have made North America so strong.

There has been some criticism, maybe harsh criticism, by others of NAFTA for decades, but we must separate the rhetoric from the facts and the criticism from people that don't have anything to do with trade. The fact is that NAFTA has benefited all three of our nations.

I encourage the administration to strengthen and modernize NAFTA. There is always room to improve it to make it better for all three countries. And we have the rare opportunity at this very time to rewrite the rules of North American trade, to make it free trade and fair trade. We must take the opportunity to write them for the better.

I believe it is important to the U.S. economy and national security that, throughout the renegotiations, the administration focuses on reaching an agreement that promotes free trade as well. We are sending a message to our current and future trading partners throughout this renegotiation. The U.S. should send a strong signal to support not only the NAFTA free trade agreement but free trade with other countries, as well, that want to trade with the U.S.

A strong U.S. economy depends on a strong framework of free trade, and I look forward to hearing from our witnesses on how the administration can strengthen NAFTA and make it better.

I will now yield to the gentleman from Massachusetts, Mr. Keating, former prosecutor—maybe still a prosecutor—for his opening statement.

[The prepared statement of Mr. Poe follows:]

Opening Statement of the Honorable **Ted Poe (R-TX), Chairman**
Subcommittee on Terrorism, Nonproliferation, and Trade Hearing:
"The Future of the North American Free Trade Agreement"
December 12, 2017

(As prepared for delivery)

23 years ago, the North American Free Trade Agreement revolutionized trade and investment between the U.S., Canada, and Mexico. We share thousands of miles of border with Canada and Mexico. They are our neighbors and our natural partners in trade and security. This partnership has been shaped by NAFTA.

I am a strong supporter of free trade. America's strength is closely connected to its economic well-being. When we break down trade barriers, American trade and American jobs increase. Trade is the lifeblood of my great home state of Texas. Last year in Texas almost one million jobs were supported by trade. Texas has been the top exporting state in the U.S. for 14 consecutive years. The overwhelming majority of Texas exporters are not big corporations: 93% percent of Texas exporters are small-and medium-sized businesses. In my district in Houston, over half of the economy depends on trade. Houston has one of the largest ports in the world and is the oil and gas capital of the world. And guess where we Texans export the most – Mexico and Canada. Our NAFTA partners.

But, Texas is just one of the many states that rely on NAFTA to fuel its economy. Study after study has shown that increased trade leads to increased jobs for Americans. More jobs mean more wealth for the average American citizen. NAFTA supports 14 million U.S. jobs. Thanks to NAFTA, trade between the U.S., Mexico, and Canada has tripled. Nearly every industry is affected in one way or another by NAFTA. The U.S. economy needs a strong NAFTA.

But free trade agreements like NAFTA do more than just grow our economy. Trade is one of our best tools of foreign policy. We have seen the connection between free trade and freedom, opportunity, and prosperity again and again. When we signed NAFTA, Mexico was a developing country. Its economy was one of the most closed in the world. Now, thanks in part to NAFTA, Mexico has an open economy valued at $2.2 trillion. This growth has made Mexico a more stable neighbor. This increased trade between our three countries has also deepened our ties with Mexico and Canada, allowing us to work together on many critical issues. Today, we cooperate with the Mexican government on issues of border security, immigration, and the fight against organized crime and drug trafficking. Our southern border security depends on our joint efforts with Mexico. Cooperation with Canada also improved due to NAFTA. Our forces train and work together to defend North America. We fight side by side against national security threats like ISIS and partner as NATO members. These are some of the most critical issues to our national security and to the security of our world.

That brings me to the reason we are all here today. To address the renegotiation of this critical free trade agreement. A lot has changed in 23 years. The internet has transformed the way companies do business. Reforms in Mexico have created new opportunities for U.S. businesses. The renegotiation presents an opportunity to update the agreement in areas like energy, e-commerce, customs and trade facilitation, and many others to strengthen and promote trade.

While there is a lot of opportunity to strengthen the agreement, there is also the risk of hurting U.S. businesses and workers. Hundreds of thousands of jobs across North America could be at risk if we pull out of NAFTA, or if we weaken the agreement. We could also do damage to our partnerships with Mexico and Canada that have made North America so strong.

There has been harsh criticism of NAFTA for decades. But we must separate the rhetoric from the facts. The fact is that NAFTA has benefited all three of our countries. So, I encourage the administration to strengthen and modernize NAFTA. There is always room for improvement. We have a rare opportunity here to rewrite the rules of North American trade. But we must take this opportunity to rewrite them for the better.

It is important to the U.S. economy and national security that throughout the renegotiations the administration focuses on reaching an agreement that promotes free trade. We are sending a message to our current and future trading partners through this renegotiation. The U.S. should send a strong signal of our support for free trade. A strong U.S. economy depends on a strong framework for free trade. I look forward to hearing from our witnesses how the administration can strengthen NAFTA.

———————

Mr. KEATING. Thank you, Mr. Chairman. Thank you, Chairman Poe, and thank you for having this hearing today.

We are here in the Subcommittee on Terrorism, Nonproliferation, and Trade, and, as anyone who watches the news knows, there are many threats facing us today in these areas: ISIS, lone-wolf attacks, escalating tensions with North Korea, and the threat, again, of nuclear war. We must be vigilant in addressing every threat here at home and in the globalized world.

The threats that cross borders and affect all of us are important. Threats from terrorism and proliferation of nuclear weapons are sobering. We must do everything in our power to keep Americans safe. But, additionally, we cannot afford to lose sight of trade. It doesn't command as much attention in the news as some of these issues I have just mentioned, but it affects every single American.

Trade has the power to affect where jobs are located, to affect wages, to affect the cost of goods and services we rely on every day without even thinking about trade policies that affect them when they are in front of us. Trade is an incredible economic and foreign policy tool if it is wielded effectively and responsibly. It is the duty of U.S. Government to take full advantage of every tool at our disposal to make life better and easier for everyday, hardworking Americans.

In order to do that in trade, we must be extremely careful in examining who wins and who loses. There has been a similar debate raging in this country over winners and losers recently, and that is over taxes. There are a lot of numbers and mathematical formulas and technical terms being thrown around with these issues, but, at the end of the day, how sure are we that it is the student, the assembly-line worker, the farmer, the mother of three, how sure are we that they are seeing the benefits of these policies?

The good news is that there are things we can do in trade so that all boats rise, because our economies, our security, our institutions are all stronger when the people at the receiving end of trade and tax and any policy, for that matter, are stronger.

However, we also have to be honest about what that means, because in trade this is not the norm. It is going to take real work to renegotiate NAFTA so that Americans, Mexicans, and Canadians see the benefits of what an effective, responsible trade policy should look like.

Unfortunately, on this issue, which will have a significant impact on each and every American's bottom line every month, I remain unconvinced that this President has approached this issue with the seriousness it demands.

For starters, the unrealistic timing parameters placed on these negotiations only suggest that the administration is willing to accept more of the same. I hope I am wrong about that, but negotiating wholesale changes in trade policy that break with long-standing trade practices takes time, no matter how quickly we might want to change that to happen and how willing we are to make sure it works toward that end.

This applies to tax, trade; it applies to anything. We should be very careful about anything that moves quickly in this city. And with very little oversight from Congress or engagement from the affected stakeholders and their representatives, this is an area of concern.

To our role in Congress, I am glad we are having this hearing in our subcommittee today, because it is a critical issue for our country and our foreign policy. We are fortunate to have our expert panel of witnesses here to inform us and inform this discussion right here in Congress on the NAFTA negotiations and what we should be paying close attention to so that we are serving the interests of the hardworking Americans in our own districts.

While I am pleased with our witnesses here today, they are not government witnesses. Our panel, they are really not the ones that are going to be in the room negotiating this when it happens. They are not negotiating in terms of the trade policy that might have the single greatest impact on our constituents during our time serving here in Congress. They are not serving at the State Department, the Office of U.S. Trade Representative, USAID, Department of Labor. They are not working in our Federal agencies tasked with taking a new NAFTA and making it function properly at all levels of implementation, down to the workers in the fields or the assembly line or the parents buying groceries.

With something of this significance, we owe it to our constituents to be fully informed on the terms that are being written into the new NAFTA, on the economic effects those terms will have on our communities back home, on what we need to do as the United States Government to make sure that everything is in place if and when a new NAFTA is signed. Because there are always risks and uncertainties when new policy is put into place, and we should work together to make sure people are not harmed in the process.

For today, with this opportunity before us, in what I hope will be the first effort at taking up the issue of NAFTA negotiations, I hope we can use this time today to learn more about what a successful renegotiation looks like. Trade is just like any other issue—tax, healthcare, financial regulation. We have learned a lot from how past practices have gone, and we have learned about who the winners and losers were under those policies. We are better not to be repeating those same mistakes. Our communities back home deserve better.

I yield back.

Mr. POE. I thank the gentleman from Massachusetts.

Without objection, all of the witnesses' prepared statements will be made part of the record.

I ask that each witness keep your presentation to no more than 5 minutes. And there is an easy way to know how long 5 minutes has passed because a red button will blink in front of you. But we do have all of your testimony, all members have your testimony, and your bios as well.

I will introduce briefly each witness and let them make their testimony.

Eric Farnsworth is the vice president of the Council of the Americas. He previously worked at the State Department, Office of the U.S. Trade Representative, and was a senior adviser to the White House Special Envoy for the Americas.

Thank you, Mr. Farnsworth, for being here.

Mr. Daniel Allford has been the president and owner of ARC Specialties of Houston, Texas, for 35 years. ARC Specialties began as a one-man operation and has grown into an internationally recognized automation company that employs 65 engineers and craftsmen.

Mr. Allford, thank you for being here and taking time away from your business.

Ambassador John Negroponte is the vice chairman of McLarty Associates. He was previously the Deputy National Security Advisor under President Reagan and was the first Director of National Intelligence under President George W. Bush. In addition, he served as the Ambassador to Honduras, Mexico, Philippines, the U.N., and Iraq.

Ms. Celeste Drake is a trade and globalization policy specialist for the American Federation of Labor and Congress of Industrial Organizations. Previously, Ms. Drake worked for Congresswoman Sanchez and Congressman Doggett, in addition to serving on the Advisory Committee for the U.S. Export-Import Bank from 2013 to 2016.

Mr. Farnsworth, we will start with you. You have 5 minutes.

STATEMENT OF MR. ERIC FARNSWORTH, VICE PRESIDENT, COUNCIL OF THE AMERICAS

Mr. FARNSWORTH. Thank you very much, Mr. Chairman. And good afternoon to you, Mr. Ranking Member, and members of the subcommittee. It is a real privilege to have the opportunity to appear before all of you to discuss the future of NAFTA.

If I may, let me give you the bottom line first. NAFTA was a true innovation in economic relations. It was designed to increase trade and investment among its three parties, promote North American economic integration, and support a vision of open-market democracy for Mexico, providing that nation with a clear path toward political and economic development. It has succeeded on all three metrics, promoting our strategic, economic, and foreign policy interests as well as our values.

Ending NAFTA would be a significant, lasting, and wholly unnecessary strategic mistake. At the same time, it is inevitable that after a quarter-century NAFTA has become dated and can usefully be modernized. And there is a landing zone, if the parties would like to achieve it.

Since 1993, U.S. trade in goods and services with Canada and Mexico increased from $307 billion to well over $1 trillion by 2016. Annual trade between the United States and Canada has more than doubled. With Mexico, trade has quadrupled. Canada is the top trading partner of the United States, and Mexico is our second-largest export market and third-largest trading partner. More than 40 U.S. States count either Canada or Mexico as their top export destination.

NAFTA has expanded trade and investment while organizing the majority of North American economic relations under a rules-based framework. As China continues its inexorable march up the development ladder and becomes increasingly economically assertive, our ability to compete economically will be further enhanced from a North America platform rather than the United States alone.

Perhaps more importantly, NAFTA institutionalized a vision for North America that would have been impossible absent significant political and economic reforms in Mexico, both catalyzing such reforms and also benefiting from them. NAFTA has directly supported Mexico's democratic transformation while also establishing a framework of trust, supporting close U.S. cooperation across a range of security issues, including counternarcotics, counterterrorism, and migration. Such cooperation is at risk if the United States continues on its current path.

Negotiations to revise NAFTA are now well underway. Press reports indicate that the most difficult issues remain to be addressed. Unless they are soon resolved, the possibility is increasing that talks may break down altogether and that the U.S. might consider giving notice of withdrawal.

According to The Wall Street Journal, some 80 percent of economists surveyed anticipate withdrawing from NAFTA would depress U.S. growth, even as Congress is right now pushing forward on a tax package designed to kickstart growth. Withdrawal would also reduce growth in both Canada and Mexico, perhaps leading to a recession and creating economic conditions that traditionally cause migration, especially from Mexico to the United States.

Much depends on the outcome of discussions surrounding rules of origin as a means to address the trade balance, although other significant issues also remain, including a sunset provision proposal and disagreements on intellectual property, government procurement, and dispute settlement procedures. Backward steps on these issues would cause irreparable damage to fully integrated supply chains and the workers whose jobs depend on them, in part because companies would find it difficult, if not impossible, to meet the required rules of origin currently under discussion.

Were NAFTA to be eliminated, the parties to the agreement would then return to previous bound tariff rates, Mexico's being far higher than ours. Agriculture exports would suffer immediately, giving up the significant advantage that has turned Mexico into the U.S.' second-largest—$18 billion—market, after only Canada.

Meanwhile, to escape tariff barriers raised by Mexico, those seeking to supply Mexico's growing market and increasingly middle-class population, may, in fact, seek to move production to Mexico. This is exactly the opposite of the intended result.

Having said all of this, the uncertainty that has been caused by the negotiations has already had negative consequences. Doubts will linger about whether the word of the United States, even one that is confirmed on a bipartisan basis by both houses of Congress, can be fully trusted again. Were we intentionally to seek ways to undermine our own global strategic interest, we might not find a better means of doing so than this.

The challenges that face the United States at this moment are significant and they are real, but NAFTA is not the culprit. Rather, the relaunch of an updated and modernized NAFTA, fully acknowledging the rapid technological advances that continue to be made, informed by a vision of a more economically integrated North America to compete effectively on a global stage, is part of the solution.

And, in the meantime, the strong, public, timely assertion by Congress of institutional prerogatives on trade and NAFTA, in particular, would be a welcome and, in my view, appropriate step.

So I want to thank you again, Judge Poe and the ranking minority member, for the opportunity to be with you today, and I look forward to your questions.

[The prepared statement of Mr. Farnsworth follows:]

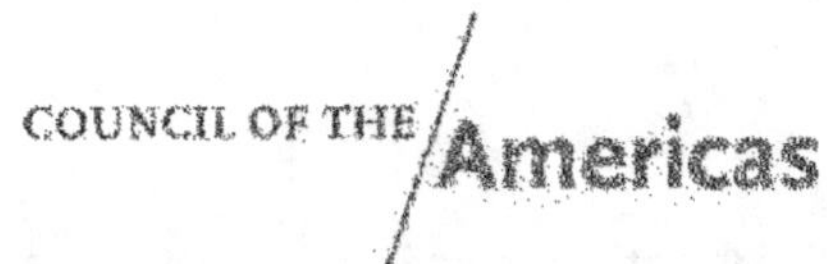

THE FUTURE OF THE NORTH AMERICAN
FREE TRADE AGREEMENT

HEARING BEFORE THE U.S. HOUSE OF REPRESENTATIVES
COMMITTEE ON FOREIGN AFFAIRS
SUBCOMMITTEE ON TERRORISM, NONPROLIFERATION,
AND TRADE
DECEMBER 12, 2017

ERIC FARNSWORTH
VICE PRESIDENT
COUNCIL OF THE AMERICAS

*** As Prepared for Delivery ***

Good afternoon, Mr. Chairman, Mr. Ranking Member, and Members. It is both a pleasure and a privilege to join you and the other distinguished panelists for today's discussion on the future of NAFTA. Thank you for the opportunity to testify on such a timely and important topic, and thank you for your leadership in highlighting these important issues from both a trade and also a security perspective.

For over 50 years the Council of the Americas has been dedicated to the promotion of democracy, open markets, and the rule of law across the Americas. We strongly believe that U.S. economic, security, and foreign policy interests are best supported with the enlightened engagement of the private sector. We also believe strongly that agreements that expand trade and investment, enlarge consumer choice and utility, create jobs in the formal sector, and promote values we share are some of the best tools that the United States maintains in order to promote sound, meaningful, and lasting engagement in the Americas and worldwide on a mutually-beneficial basis.

<u>NAFTA is a Success in Economic and Foreign Policy</u>

Mr. Chairman and Members of the Subcommittee, let me give you the bottom line first: NAFTA was a true innovation in economic relations. It was designed to increase trade and investment among its three parties; promote North American economic integration; and support a vision of open market democracy for Mexico providing that nation with a clear path toward political and economic modernization. It has succeeded on all three metrics, promoting our strategic, economic, and foreign policy interests, as well as our values. Ending NAFTA would be a significant, lasting, and wholly unnecessary strategic mistake.

At the same time, it is inevitable that after almost a quarter century NAFTA has become dated and can usefully be modernized. In attempting to do so, all three parties to the agreement must understand what is truly at stake if they are unable to come to satisfactory agreement. Mending NAFTA is appropriate, and there is a landing zone if the parties want to achieve it.

Since 1993, U.S. trade in goods and services with Canada and Mexico increased from $307 billion to well over $1 *trillion* by 2016. Annual trade between the United States and Canada has more than doubled; with Mexico trade has quadrupled. Canada is the top trading partner of the United States and Mexico is our second largest export market and third largest trading partner. More than 40 states count either Canada or Mexico as their top export destination. Perhaps more importantly, beyond these tangible commercial benefits, NAFTA institutionalized a vision for North America that would have been impossible absent significant political and economic reforms in Mexico, both catalyzing such reforms and also benefitting from them. As China continues its inexorable march up the development ladder and becomes increasingly economically assertive, our ability to compete will continue to be enhanced from a North America platform rather than the United States alone.

In addition, agreements like NAFTA are not just about trade and investment, they are also critical if often under-appreciated tools of US foreign policy and the promotion of our values. Unquestionably, NAFTA has directly supported Mexico's democratic transformation. It required legislative and regulatory changes that might not otherwise have occurred absent an external catalyst. It has also empowered new economic constituencies and a growing middle class that has demanded and received an increasingly clear political voice. Arguably, Mexico's politics are more transparent and democratic today than ever before, and the Mexican people have made clear their disinterest in returning to the ways of the past. And NAFTA also established a framework of trust, built on stability and long-run commitment, supporting close U.S. cooperation with Mexico across a range of security issues including counter narcotics and counter terrorism, in addition to meaningful assistance to address migration flows that continue from Central America. (Net migration from Mexico itself to the United States has become virtually zero as Mexico's economy generates new opportunities for its workers). A full accounting of NAFTA's impact cannot overlook these critically important issues.

At the same time, NAFTA has done much to enhance confidence in the United States. Recent actions and rhetoric that stigmatize Mexicans or that are perceived as anti-Mexico, including inflexible NAFTA negotiating positions that are politically impossible for Mexico and also Canada to adopt, are leading to a revival of a more strident, traditional anti-U.S. posture that has taken a generation of goodwill on all sides to overcome. As Mexicans in particular go to the polls in 2018 to elect their next president, such matters will not be far from their minds and may impact both the final outcome as well as the political space that the new president, whoever he or she is, will have to cooperate with the United States on a multitude of issues—including security, counter narcotics, and immigration—going forward.

<u>The World has Changed Since 1994, and NAFTA has Become Dated</u>

From the trade perspective, NAFTA was at the cutting edge when it was passed originally. Heretofore there had never been an effort to link the world's largest, most developed economy with an economically backward, underdeveloped neighbor that seemed to lurch from economic crisis to crisis. The gulf between Mexico and its two other North American neighbors was large and perhaps insurmountable over the near term. At the same time, the pre-existing free trade agreement that the United States had already implemented with Canada was cause for Ottawa to join the talks as a defensive move, so as not to see their own benefits eroded by a U.S. agreement with Mexico. Along with certain constitutional and political restrictions in all three countries, this meant that negotiators could move ahead only so far, excluding certain sectors such as energy because they were too politically controversial at the time. What the negotiators created, however, proved to be an effective framework for ordering the majority of North American trade and investment relations during the economic stresses, political transitions, and security crises of the past 23, almost 24 years.

Since then, however, the world has changed dramatically, and NAFTA is now showing its age and should be modernized. Three long-term trends must be highlighted, all of which continue apace even after the U.S. elections just over a year ago.

First, production models have evolved. Canada, Mexico, and the United States do not merely trade products as we did when NAFTA was first implemented; we now design and make them together. In many industries, joint production and supply chains have developed to such an extent that, from the commercial perspective at least, national borders no longer define products. This is to our benefit: according to the National Bureau of Economic Statistics, every dollar of U.S. imports from Mexico, for example, includes some 40 percent of U.S. content; for Canada it is 25 percent. As a result it is no longer accurate to think in terms of U.S. or Mexican or Canadian products when North America itself has become the production platform. North America has become a true 21st century economic space, just in time to compete more effectively with China, India, and others. As former Under Secretary of Commerce Stefan Selig has just written, putting America first therefore means putting North America first.

Second, consider that in 1994, there was barely an internet, much less Facebook or Twitter. Nobody knew how radically and rapidly electronic communications would fundamentally alter business models around the world. But it's not just email and social media. Consider the incredible advances that technology has made possible in the auto and manufacturing sectors, energy, financial services, IT, medical products, agriculture, and virtually every other economic sector in the past two plus decades. Entire industries that were not even contemplated by NAFTA are now a significant part of all three economies. The original NAFTA could not possibly have anticipated these developments and a renegotiated NAFTA could potentially provide an opportunity to include them within the framework of an updated and more fully comprehensive regional agreement. In addition, it would allow the inclusion of sectors such as energy heretofore excluded for political reasons.

Third, there was a noticeable change in trade patterns within North America demarcated by 9/11, at which point the border "thickened" and commercial activities understandably took a second seat to security. A resulting lack of sufficient attention to commercial needs at the borders, specifically in cross-border infrastructure but in other areas too, created unnecessary bottlenecks and wait times for commercial traffic that erode the compelling advantages of geographic proximity. Some work has been done since then, but as NAFTA-facilitated trade increases, infrastructure has not kept up. And it goes without saying that building additional walls and barricades could only exacerbate the bottlenecks that already exist and which are so much unnecessary pressure on the a windpipe of the U.S. economy. Modernizing the agreement could also provide an excellent opportunity to take a more balanced look at border issues.

<u>Which Future Are We Working to Create?</u>

Negotiations to revise NAFTA beginning in August are now well underway. Five rounds have been concluded; a sixth is scheduled for January in Montreal, and negotiators are meeting right now in Washington for an interim "intercessional" gathering. Press reports indicate that the most difficult issues remain to be addressed even as negotiators race to try to conclude talks by the end of the first quarter, 2018, consistent with Mexico's pending election campaign process.

Unless the most difficult issues are soon resolved, however, the possibility is increasing that talks may break down altogether and that the U.S. might consider withdrawal. Such a result would have meaningful negative consequences for the United States, to say nothing of the damage it would also inflict on our two closest neighbors Canada and Mexico. It would be a strategic setback for the United States.

According to the Wall Street Journal, some 80 percent of economists surveyed anticipate that a withdrawal from NAFTA would depress U.S. growth, even as Congress is right now pushing forward on a tax package designed to kick-start growth. Withdrawal would also reduce growth in both Canada and Mexico, perhaps leading to recession and creating economic conditions that are traditionally the primary cause of migration especially from Mexico to the United States. And, it would mean the abandonment of dispute resolution mechanisms that have worked for the United States, risking a return to the days when the resolution of disputes is driven primarily by politics rather than rules-based systems.

Much depends on the outcome of discussions surrounding rules of origin as a means to "fix" the trade balance, although other significant issues also remain including an ill-advised sunset provision proposal and disagreements on intellectual property, government procurement, and dispute settlement procedures. A singular focus on the trade balance in goods neglects the healthy trade surplus that the United States enjoys under NAFTA in services. But, more significantly, backward steps on these issues would also cause irreparable damage to fully integrated supply chains and the workers whose jobs depend on them, in part because companies would find it difficult if not impossible to meet the required rules of origin currently under discussion.

Assuming that agreement can even be found around these issues, steps the Administration is proposing to raise rules of origin requirements substantially would cause a re-evaluation by producers whether to utilize NAFTA provisions or whether to skip NAFTA altogether and utilize less onerous provisions. Domestic job creation could actually suffer as production is shifted elsewhere.

Meanwhile, the elimination of NAFTA would allow the parties to the agreement to return to previous bound tariff rates, Mexico's being far higher than ours. Agriculture exports would suffer immediately, giving up the significant advantage that has turned Mexico in the U.S.' second largest, $18 billion market in agriculture, after only Canada. This is a market that can rapidly be filled by other globally-competitive producers, an overwhelming potential loss particularly for agricultural producers already hammered by lower commodities prices and income.

To escape tariff barriers raised by Mexico in a post-NAFTA environment, those seeking to supply Mexico's growing market and increasingly middle-class population, predicted to be a top-seven global economy by 2050, may seek to produce in Mexico rather than the United States. This would also allow them to avail themselves of Mexico's impressive network of trade agreements that has turned the nation into a global production powerhouse. Mexico's recent energy and other reforms have brought down manufacturing costs further, making the nation still more competitive. As a result, rather than returning production to the United States, such an outcome would actually threaten to create incentives for a migration of production from the United States to Mexico and also Canada. This is exactly opposite the intended result.

Having said all of this, even if final agreement is reached at some point in the New Year, the uncertainty that has been caused by the negotiations process has already had negative consequences. In addition to investments that have been delayed, and therefore jobs that have not been created, our closest allies and trading partners now have reason to question the reliability of the United States over the longer term. We would join the likes of others, such as Venezuela, that have unilaterally abrogated existing trade and investment agreements, followed by years of economic trials and unending legal actions.

Trust in U.S. intentions and dependability as an ally is a precious commodity, and goes well beyond trade agreements. Once lost it is unlikely to be regained at the same level for many years, perhaps ever. Doubts will linger about whether the word of the United States, even one that is confirmed on a bipartisan basis by both Houses of Congress, can ever be fully trusted again. The United States is diminished. Were we to intentionally seek ways to undermine our own global strategic interests, we might not find a better means of doing so than this.

The economic and political challenges that face that United States at this moment in time are significant. They are not to be understated or ignored. They must be addressed, effectively and soon, with sensitivity and grace, particularly for those of our citizens who may have been left behind by the global economy. But NAFTA is not the culprit, and ending NAFTA will not bring back an earlier time nor will it provide U.S. leverage to promote the values that we hold dear, including environmental protections and labor rights.

Rather, the relaunch of an updated and modernized NAFTA fully acknowledging the rapid technological advances that continue to be made, informed by a vision of a more economically integrated North America to compete effectively on the global stage, will be the far better option. This would also allow us the means to intensify the promotion of stronger environmental protects and labor rights, which we would actually lose altogether without the existence of NAFTA. And in the meantime, the strong, public assertion by Congress of its institutional prerogatives on trade and NAFTA in particular, well in advance of any irrevocable and precipitous decision made by the United States, would be a welcome and appropriate, even necessary, step.

Thank you, again, Mr. Chairman, for the opportunity to be with you today, and I look forward to your questions.

Mr. POE. Thank you, Mr. Farnsworth.

Mr. Allford?

STATEMENT OF MR. DANIEL ALLFORD, PRESIDENT, ARC SPECIALTIES

Mr. ALLFORD. Mr. Poe and members of the Terrorism, Non-proliferation, and Trade Subcommittee of the Committee on Foreign Affairs, thank you for inviting me today to talk on NAFTA.

I am Dan Allford, president of ARC Specialties in Houston, Texas. We design, program, and build automated machines and robots used around the world.

I started in 1983 in Houston when I built a hot tap welding machine for a plutonium processing plant in Idaho. I have always suspected that if the customer had known it was a young man in his garage building this they might have been a little bit worried. However, it worked so well, we built another one in the 1990s.

The business grew out of the garage around 1990, and, over the last 35 years, we have engineered and built hundreds of machines that are operating in 25 countries on 6 continents. We now occupy over 100,000 square feet of engineering and manufacturing space and employ 65 engineers and craftsmen.

I have personally worked in and observed the market systems in 15 different countries. This experience has made me an enthusiastic free-market capitalist.

ARC Specialties has always built machinery used for the manufacture of equipment used in the exploration and refining operations in the energy industry. In 2015, when oil prices crashed and the Houston economy slowed, we needed new markets. We found that the solutions we had developed to solve oil industry problems worked equally well in other industries around the world.

Since the beginning of 2015, we have designed, built, and shipped machines to Canada, Mexico, Romania, Singapore, Oman, Saudi Arabia, China, India, France, and the U.K. exports have account for 30 percent of our revenues. Canada and Mexico accounted for half of our exports. In the process, we have learned to deal with trade barriers ranging from red tape to tariffs.

Most of my knowledge of NAFTA comes from personal experience doing business across the globe. My experience is that NAFTA has helped us sell machines in Mexico and Canada. I sincerely believe that the free-market system used here in the United States is a major contributor to the success and productivity of our country. Tariffs and subsidies distort markets and degrade efficiency. A free market and a level playing field bring out the best in people by rewarding their efforts. I firmly agree with the adage that competition breeds excellence.

In 1960, one transistor cost $4. Now, $4 will purchase 1 billion transistors. This is the result of the free market encouraging technological improvements through automation. The whole process is driven by fair competition. I don't fear competition. I relish the challenge.

I can beat the competition, but I can't beat the tariff. The United States innovates, others duplicate, and the cycle starts over, and everyone benefits from increased productivity. Better products are made available to consumers at lower prices.

What I do fear is an unfair environment. Tariffs and red tape on one side tend to create reciprocal tariffs and red tape on the other. Technical problems can be solved using engineering and ingenuity, while tariffs create political and administrative cost barriers that restrict trade.

I export machines to Brazil, where Brazilian tariffs can add as much as 40 percent to the cost of my equipment. This is counter-productive for all parties. These machines are used to apply welded internal coatings to valves and pipes used in the oil industry. These coatings create a corrosion-resistant barrier to the hydrogen sulfide or sour gas present in Brazilian crude and help prevent catastrophic failures and oil spills. Brazilian tariffs make my machines unaffordable for most companies. These tariffs cost my company revenues and cost the U.S. jobs. I fear the same thing will occur in Mexico and Canada if changes are made to NAFTA that distort the free-market system.

I believe that everyone should have an opportunity to work and provide for their family. This is a great stabilizer in the world. In a free-market system, prices for goods and services are determined by the open market and consumers. A free market works when the laws and forces of supply and demands are unhindered by government intervention.

I am proud to be involved in manufacturing because it is one of the few segments of our economy that creates wealth. Our robots and machines help U.S. companies compete in a global economy, and our exports of equipment help the balance of trade.

I am honored to be here today, and I ask you to help me to continue to create jobs in the United States of America by encouraging international free trade.

[The prepared statement of Mr. Allford follows:]

The North American Free Trade Agreement and its Effect on a Texas Robotics Manufacturer

Daniel Allford

President

ARC Specialties Inc.

Testimony Submitted to the Subcommittee on Terrorism, Nonproliferation and Trade, House Committee on Foreign Affairs

December 12, 2017

The North American Free Trade Agreement passed congress in 1993 with strong bipartisan support. It went into effect in 1994. Since then trade between the U.S., Mexico and Canada has more than tripled. This is the same time period during which my company began exporting our U.S. designed and built machines around the world. As a machinery and robotics manufacturer we have benefited from sales to Mexico and Canada. Mexico needed machines for new manufacturing plants and Canada needed machines to build oilfield equipment for their oil industry. Unhindered by tariffs ARC Specialties was well positioned to supply these machines which enabled ARC to grow and provide jobs for U.S. citizens.

Industrial machinery, machine tools and robotics are used across the world in manufacturing. We have shipped automated manufacturing equipment and robots to 25 counties. We have encountered various trade barriers when exporting machines internationally. In Europe we were forced to comply with cumbersome certification requirements which entail $30,000 in compliance testing on each new design. In Russia there was endless red tape. In China the certification process is tedious and tends to reveal proprietary product designs. In most of the countries where we installed machines, tariffs made our products much more expensive than domestic units. In Brazil these tariffs could reach 40% of the price of the machine. In spite of tariffs we sold machines in countries around the world, including Brazil, but in smaller numbers. Each country offered unique challenges with two exceptions: Mexico and Canada. I attribute this to NAFTA and therefore I believe that the agreement should remain in force and any changes should be vetted to ensure that free trade remains unhindered.

One of the commercial advantages of the United States is the size of our country and the diversity of our population, thus creating opportunities through the division of labor. Specialization works because interstate trade in the US is nearly effortless. Trade allows each of us to do what we do best. NAFTA provides the same advantage by essentially eliminating almost all tariffs among the three nations, and allowing for the seamless flow of goods and supplies across borders.

NAFTA did not come without a price. Some jobs shifted to Mexico due to lower wages, consistent with historical trends. In the 1960s jobs shifted to Japan. Once Japanese wages rose, jobs shifted to China and more recently to India, Vietnam and other countries. The United States innovates. Other countries duplicate, then the cycle starts over and everyone benefits by increased productivity. When goods are produced at lower labor rates, Americans benefit by paying lower prices for electronics, cars, clothes and food. Lower prices are always the goal of manufacturers seeking a market advantage. Lower prices due to improved efficiency are an indication of progress. Productivity is a ratio of production output to what is required to produce it. Americans vote with their pocket book every time they look for lower prices.

When mature industries shift production to low cost labor countries this frees up capital and talent in the US to create new products and new industries. In 1900 over 40% of our population worked in agriculture, now less than 2 % do. Agriculture is the first automation success story. We never hear anyone complain about lower food prices or year around availability of fresh fruits and vegetables. No one has lamented to me that he would rather be plowing a field behind a horse. I don't believe that the U.S. jobs lost to Mexico and Asia are the necessarily the jobs we want in the future. Trade creates jobs. The U.S. Chamber of Commerce estimates that about 14 million U.S. jobs depend on trade with Mexico and Canada.[1]

As a Houston company we are primarily involved in the energy industry. NAFTA has had a substantial and positive impact on the energy sector. The North American energy market is highly integrated and interdependent. Heavy crude oil from Canada and Mexico flows to the US where it is well suited for Midwest and Gulf refineries. Canada and Mexico now account for half of our total energy imports reducing dependency on less reliable and frequently hostile alternatives. In the US this crude is refined, adding value and some is exported back to both countries. This is the free market efficiently allocating resources. Each trading partner supplies what they can produce efficiently and purchases what they cannot.

The benefits to the energy markets including oil, natural gas, and electricity provided by NAFTA, as supported by the American Petroleum Institute (API), also benefit equipment manufacturers in the US. [2]

ARC Specialties has built automated manufacturing equipment for companies in both Canada and Mexico. These machines are used in the produce equipment for the production oil and gas that may be imported into the US for processing in US refineries.

According to the National Association of Manufacturers, 2016 exports of manufactured goods to Canada and Mexico equaled the total of the next 10 largest trading partners.[3] In the last three years my ratio was very similar. Half of my exports were to Canada and Mexico. U.S. exports to Canada and Mexico supported the jobs of 2 million men and women at 43,000 firms across the United States. These jobs paid an average wage of $81,289 which is 27% higher than the overall average nonfarm wage. Export related jobs pay an average of 18 to 20% more than jobs not related to exports. At a minimum everyone in the world deserves the opportunity to work and provide for themselves and their families. This is a great stabilizer in society.

The Department of Commerce, International Trade Administration states that in 2015 Mexico was the largest export market for US machine tool manufacturers eclipsing China in both cutting and forming machine tool sales.[4] ARC Specialties is one of the last remaining manufacturers of large industrial robots in the United States. For ARC Specialties the loss of our two largest export markets due to tariffs would be devastating.

Much of the impetus for withdrawal from NAFTA comes from the U.S. auto industry. Most studies have shown that NAFTA benefits the auto industry. The Motor and Equipment Manufacturers Association commissioned a study by The Boston Consulting Group on the "Impact of BAT and NAFTA Reforms on the U.S. Motor Vehicle Industry".[5] This study concludes that "the economics of reshoring are not favorable for most motor vehicle products" and that "production in Mexico still more economical in the event of a border adjustment tax". Withdrawal from NAFTA with a 35% tariff would result in an increase of ~$1,200 per vehicle passed on to the consumer. The study states that "access to NAFTA low cost production is critical to compete in the global market". Germany relies on low-cost production in nearby Eastern Europe to keep cost down.

Ironically one probable response by automakers and consumers will be to "decrease content" or strip features to avoid cost increases. This decrease in content is predicted to cause the loss of 20 to 50k U.S. manufacturing jobs from the current 870k U.S. supplier employees. Charles Uthus at the American Automotive Policy Council said that the demise of NAFTA would be "basically a $10 billion tax on the auto industry in America"

Withdrawing from NAFTA would have an even greater effect on U.S. Agriculture which exported $38B to Mexico in 2016. Reverting to pre NAFTA tariffs levels would result in 75% duties on chicken and corn syrup, 45% on turkey, potatoes and dairy products and 15% on wheat.[6]

While working in former USSR countries I witnessed the devastating effect that central planning has on markets. When governments pick winners with subsidies and trade barriers, everyone else in the market loses. Quality declines, innovation stalls, service is degraded and prices are distorted.

In conclusion the North American Free Trade Agreement works. It stimulates trade and creates jobs. As a manufacturer who imports and exports, I believe that it is important to remain in NAFTA. I am proud to be involved with manufacturing because it is one of the few segments of our economy which creates wealth. Our robots and machines enable US companies to compete in a global economy and our exports of equipment help the balance of trade. I hope you will help me to continue to create wealth and create jobs in the United States of America by encouraging international free trade.

---

[1] https://www.uschamber.com/sites/default/files/legacy/reports/1112_INTL_NAFTA_20Years.pdf

[2] http://www.api.org/~/media/Files/Policy/Trade/North-American-Energy-Onepager.pdf

[3] http://www.nam.org/Issues/Trade/North-America-Drives-Manufacturing-in-the-United-States-and-a-Modernized-NAFTA-Would-Further-Boost-US-Jobs-and-Exports/

[4] www.trade.gov/topmarkets

[5] https://www.mema.org/sites/default/files/BCG%20MEMA%20BAT%20NAFTA%20Study%20Summary.pdf

[6] https://www.wsj.com/articles/trumps-nafta-threat-1508105756

Mr. POE. Thank you, Mr. Allford. Well said.
Ambassador?

STATEMENT OF THE HONORABLE JOHN D. NEGROPONTE, VICE CHAIRMAN, MCLARTY ASSOCIATES (FORMER DEPUTY SECRETARY OF STATE AND FORMER DIRECTOR OF NATIONAL INTELLIGENCE)

Mr. NEGROPONTE. Thank you. Thank you, Chairman Poe——
Mr. POE. Your microphone.
Mr. NEGROPONTE. Oh, sorry. I should have remembered at least that. I haven't been out of government that long.

Thank you to Chairman Poe and Ranking Member Keating and other members of this subcommittee for inviting me to testify at this hearing on NAFTA, a topic that has long been of personal and professional interest and that is highly relevant for Congress at this critical juncture. NAFTA's modernization is both necessary and important.

For my part, I am proud to say that I have been an advocate for transforming North America into a more competitive economic force for decades. During my time as United States Ambassador to Mexico, I had the privilege to be involved in NAFTA's conception and negotiation. When I went down to Mexico, our trade relationship was modest and the United States-Mexico political relationship was frequently fraught. "Distant Neighbors" was the title of the book that best described our bilateral interaction.

Through NAFTA, we hoped to be able to integrate our economies in a way that would benefit all three countries and allow us to better compete, including with Asia and with the countries of Eastern Europe that were emerging after the fall of the Soviet Union.

I will never forget my meeting with President George H.W. Bush and Secretary of State James Baker where I walked through the pros and cons of having a NAFTA, an idea that they green-lighted, seeing the economic and security benefits in such a strategic alliance.

While the economic and social pressures of an increasingly globalized world have made NAFTA a controversial subject, I am of the view that NAFTA has been beneficial to our country. Its renegotiation should recognize the strategic importance of our North American partnership from both a geopolitical and economic perspective. Our work with our neighbors on law enforcement, counternarcotics, and counterterrorism are key components to keeping America safe. We simply do not have the luxury of putting this collaboration at risk.

And, economically, trade with Canada and Mexico supports millions of jobs, and our North American partners buy more U.S. manufactured goods every year than the next 10 largest markets combined. Rather than offshoring to Asia, critical supply chains have been able to remain in North America, enhancing our ability to compete.

NAFTA created unprecedented export opportunities for U.S. manufacturers, farmers, energy and service providers, small- and medium-size enterprises, and, yes, even workers, building the foundation of a closer strategic trilateral partnership.

At the same time, NAFTA has long been a punching bag, as our country has failed to effectively address the needs of communities hit by shifting market demand, enhanced globalization, and technology. These are pressing matters that we must take head-on. But withdrawing from NAFTA to attempt to address these issues is like putting a splint on your arm to try to heal a broken leg. It is not likely to work. The uncertainty created by withdrawal benefits no one, least of all the United States.

Do we need to modernize this agreement? Absolutely. The world has moved on since NAFTA's entry into force. Do we need to threaten withdrawal to do so? Absolutely not.

So what can we do? First and foremost, I think it is important that Congress exercise its prerogatives in matters concerning trade and commerce. Hopefully this hearing will be a piece of that. And my hope is that local communities threatened by a dissolution of NAFTA will help to build a national consensus for the status quo, ideally for NAFTA modernization as well.

Most importantly, I think we must rebuild a consensus not on trade necessarily but on competitiveness, on the need to ensure that the United States remains one of the most competitive economies in the world. This will mean engaging in real policy debates about the causes of economic struggle in certain parts of the country rather than turning to NAFTA as a convenient scapegoat.

Wouldn't it be ironic if it were the United States' actions that harmed the bilateral relationship with Mexico, returning us once again to being distant neighbors?

Thank you again for the opportunity to testify today. I look forward to your questions, Mr. Chairman.

[The prepared statement of Mr. Negroponte follows:]

<u>The Future of the North American Free Trade Agreement</u>

Hearing Before the Terrorism, Nonproliferation, and Trade Subcommittee
Committee on Foreign Affairs
U.S. House of Representatives

Tuesday, December 12, 2017 at 2:00pm

<u>Written Testimony of John D. Negroponte</u>
Vice Chairman, McLarty Associates

Chairman Poe, Ranking Member Keating, and distinguished members of the Committee:

Thank you for inviting me to testify at this hearing on NAFTA, a topic that has long been of personal and professional interest and that is highly relevant for Congress at this critical juncture. **Modernization of NAFTA is both necessary and important,** a fact I believe no one disputes. The absence of digital trade disciplines is the starkest example. For my part, I am proud to say that I have been an advocate for transforming North America into a more competitive economic force for decades.

During my time as U.S. Ambassador to Mexico, I had the privilege to be involved in NAFTA's conception and negotiation. People often forget how fraught the U.S.-Mexico relationship was pre-NAFTA. Anti-Americanism was the norm, but the threat of the rise of Asian economies was real. In addition, with the fall of the Soviet Union, the economies of Eastern Europe were newly emerging, seeking to attract investment. **We hoped to be able to integrate our economies in a way that would accrue to the benefit of all three countries** – the United States, Mexico and Canada – and allow us to compete better. I will never forget my meeting with President George H.W. Bush and Secretary of State James Baker where I walked through the pros and cons of having a NAFTA. It goes without saying they green-lighted the proposal, seeing the economic and security benefits in such a strategic alliance.

While the economic and social pressures of an increasingly globalized world have made NAFTA a controversial concept since its early days, I am of the view that **NAFTA has been enormously beneficial to our country.** Renegotiation should recognize the strategic importance of our partnership within North America from both an economic and a geopolitical perspective. It should recognize that – to our mutual benefit – NAFTA institutions increased labor standards in Mexico, decreased environmental degradation in border areas, and enhanced rule of law south of the border.

We are **no longer living in the era depicted in that classic tome <u>Distant Neighbors</u>,** by then-New York Times correspondent Alan Riding. Suspicion and mistrust no longer rule the day. In fact, we have increasingly developed a shared sense of **security** – which only intensified after 9/11, as I saw during my time as Director for National Intelligence.

Our work with our neighbors on law enforcement, counternarcotics, and counterterrorism are key components to keeping America safe. Canada is a steadfast ally, and the United States maintains sophisticated law enforcement collaboration and intelligence exchange with Mexico to fight money laundering and jointly combat the menace posed by organized crime. We simply do not have the luxury of putting this collaboration at risk.

Economically, fourteen million American jobs depend on trade with Canada and Mexico, by far the largest export markets for the United States. Our North American partners buy more than $600 billion in U.S. manufactured goods every year, more than the next ten largest markets combined. Since 1993, U.S. trade with Mexico has quintupled in nominal terms, while trade with the rest of the world has only tripled. Three-way trade quadrupled, creating a powerful engine for economic growth. Rather than offshoring to Asia, critical supply chains have been able to remain in North America, enhancing our country's ability to compete. U.S. **services and**

technology companies found open markets in which to operate; indeed, the United States has a services surplus in North America of $88 billion. Comparing this strategy to that of nations like Brazil, where forced local content requirements and high tariffs have ruled the day, making manufactured exports uncompetitive and local prices on items like autos and computers astronomical, the wisdom of creating a competitiveness zone in North America seems clear.

In addition, the integration of North American **energy** markets allowed the United States to decrease our reliance on energy imports from across the Atlantic, encouraging greater energy independence in the region.

In particular, NAFTA has helped U.S. **farmers** and ranchers, boosting U.S. agricultural exports by 350%. It is important to note that many U.S. states in the heartland list Canada and Mexico as their top export destinations – this is due to NAFTA. Looking at the electoral map from the last election, it is hard to overlook that these states in great measure supported the President, making consideration of a NAFTA withdrawal not only questionable economically, but politically.

Small and medium sized enterprises have also been big winners under NAFTA. Canada and Mexico have become "test markets," if you will, for smaller U.S. companies seeking to go global one step at a time. Indeed, we have seen that at my consulting firm, McLarty Associates, as we have helped companies to internationalize – the first step is almost always North America.

In short, NAFTA created unprecedented export opportunities for U.S. manufacturers, farmers, service providers, and, yes, even workers, building the foundation of a closer strategic trilateral partnership that has yielded economic and security benefits. At the same time, **NAFTA has long been a punching bag**, as our country has failed to effectively address the needs of communities hit by shifting market demand, enhanced globalization, and technology shifts. In many areas struck by job losses, workers find themselves underwater in their homes, unable to sell, unable to leave to pursue other economic opportunities. These are the pressing issues we must address. But withdrawing from NAFTA to attempt to address these issues is like putting a splint on your arm to try to heal a broken leg. It is not likely to work.

Do we need to modernize this agreement? Absolutely. The world has moved on since NAFTA's January 1, 1994, entry into force. Do we need to threaten withdrawal to do so? Absolutely not.

What we have seen with the looming threat of withdrawal is companies hedging against a possible dissolution of the agreement, thus reducing NAFTA's benefits today. Why continue to buy high-fructose corn syrup from the United States when you can lock down sugar contracts with third parties now? Why not investigate the price of Argentine wheat? This is rational economic behavior, driven by an unreasonable threat of withdrawal.

There is no doubt that the United States should come to the table ready to negotiate tough. We always do – and I can personally assure you that we did in the original NAFTA talks, as I was intimately involved. However, the uncertainty created by withdrawal benefits no one, least of all the United States. Our trading partners have already made clear that they will abandon the negotiating table if the United States moves to withdraw, and I for one do not think they are bluffing. It would be difficult to continue after being so disrespected by such an important economic and geopolitical ally.

Further, Canada and Mexico have pursued their own agreements outside of North America. Prime Minister Trudeau was in China just last week to initiate talks, and Canada recently completed its comprehensive free trade agreement with Europe, the EU-Canada Comprehensive Economic and Trade Agreement (CETA). Mexico has advanced in trade discussions with South America. As Mexico and Canada logically hedge their bets, U.S. producers, farmers, and workers lose out. With these moves, the United States risks moving from a partner of choice for Canada and Mexico to a partner when convenient.

So, what can we do? First and foremost, it is important that Congress exercise its prerogatives in matters concerning trade and commerce. Hopefully, this hearing will be an important piece of that. Given the legal uncertainties that I understand cloud any withdrawal scenario, it is imperative in my view that Congress move swiftly to protect the agreement, stressing to the Executive Branch the opportunity costs involved in putting not only the agreement but our trilateral relationships in peril.

My hope is that the local communities threatened by a dissolution of NAFTA will be educated on the matter, so at a minimum, we can build a national consensus for the status quo, ideally for NAFTA modernization as well. And lastly, but most importantly, we must rebuild a consensus not on trade necessarily, but on competitiveness – on the need to ensure that the United States remains one of the most competitive economies in the world. This will mean engaging in real policy debates about the causes of economic struggle in certain parts of the United States, rather than deploying trade and NAFTA as a convenient scapegoat.

How ironic would it be if it were our actions that seriously harmed the North American partnership, returning our relationship with Mexico once again to that of "distant neighbors."

Thank you again for the opportunity to testify today. I look forward to your questions.

*　　*　　*

Mr. POE. Thank you, Ambassador.
Ms. Drake?

STATEMENT OF MS. CELESTE DRAKE, TRADE AND GLOBALIZATION POLICY SPECIALIST, THE AMERICAN FEDERATION OF LABOR AND CONGRESS OF INDUSTRIAL ORGANIZATIONS

Ms. DRAKE. Thank you. Good afternoon, Chairman Poe, Ranking Member Keating, members of the committee.

I am pleased to testify about NAFTA on behalf of the American Federation of Labor and Congress of Industrial Organizations, representing 12½ million working people in every sector of our economy, including mining, retail, manufacturing, transportation, public service, and construction.

While CEOs and global corporations have generally benefited from NAFTA, it has failed the working people of North America. While it has increased the amount of trade between Mexico, Canada, and the United States, it has also cost jobs, depressed wages, weakened worker negotiating power, and destabilized communities across all three countries.

Trade will always be disruptive, both creating and destroying jobs, but NAFTA's rules redistributed income upwards, providing rewards to the wealthiest and most powerful, while making it tougher to succeed for the rest of us. Trade does not inevitably have to redistribute income in this manner. So if we change the rules, we can change the outcomes.

That is why today's hearing is so important. The renegotiation process that began in August is continuing even as we meet today here in Washington, DC. Unfortunately, due to the secrecy of the talks, we cannot discuss at this open hearing the specifics of the texts that each party is proposing.

But we do know some of the general outlines. Canada has been very transparent about its ambition to protect its workers from being undercut by U.S. and Mexican policies that suppress wages by limiting the negotiating power of working people. And the U.S. has been equally transparent about its proposal to limit NAFTA's special legal privileges for foreign investors, which act as a subsidy for U.S. employers who outsource to Mexico.

The AFL-CIO believes these proposals represent positive steps toward the transformation of NAFTA that is necessary to reverse its race-to-the-bottom model. We also commend Ambassador Lighthizer and his team for their willingness to consult with Labor.

But initial steps and respectful consultations are not sufficient to provide confidence that the future of NAFTA will vary from its past. To truly set up a fair and level playing field, NAFTA, in renegotiation, must address labor issues that were basically swept under the rug the first time around. NAFTA's labor and environment side deals must be replaced with clear, effective, binding rules in the core text.

Put simply, NAFTA's side agreements don't work. Over 23 years, they have done nothing to ensure that NAFTA's labor rules are monitored or enforced, including in the case of Mexico, where the government cooperates with employers and employer-dominated unions to keep wages low and workers from having an independent voice in the workplace. Indeed, just last week, two senators from Mexico's ruling party introduced a bill that would undermine constitutional amendments as well as commitments already made to the U.S.

This failure to address longstanding denials of worker rights and freedoms in Mexico is a key reason that NAFTA has not raised wages, benefits, or freedoms for North American families. If effectively addressing Mexico's entrenched system of labor repression is not part of the NAFTA renegotiation, there is little chance that it will stop hurting North American families.

For this committee, this issue is critical. Working people, not just in the United States but around the globe, have been expressing more and more doubt about the current model of globalization—not about trade, but about global economic rules that reward exploitation and pollution, that fail to protect migrant workers, that deny working families open access to global rulemaking, that provide special privileges to Wall Street banks and brand-name pharmaceutical companies, and that make the American Dream harder to reach, particularly for the two-thirds of working Americans who lack a bachelor's degree.

Congress should demand that NAFTA negotiators think bigger. Negotiators must consider how to incorporate rules that allow the U.S. to develop manufacturing policy to bring new family-wage jobs to our industrial heartland. The new NAFTA should also include rules to combat tax avoidance and promote infrastructure investments. Without such rules, disinvestment in the U.S. economy will continue to undermine productivity and the middle class.

For NAFTA to have a bright future, it must incorporate lessons learned from mistakes of the past, including the failed 9-year case against Guatemala. A new NAFTA that addresses these issues should be viewed as the first of a new line of trade deals that have the confidence of the people making the products and providing the services that are traded.

I will stop here, and I am happy to answer any questions you may have.

[The prepared statement of Ms. Drake follows:]

**BEFORE THE HOUSE SUBCOMMITTEE ON TERRORISM,
NONPROLIFERATION, AND TRADE
OF THE COMMITTEE ON FOREIGN AFFAIRS**

HEARING ON

**"THE FUTURE OF THE NORTH AMERICAN
FREE TRADE AGREEMENT"**

TESTIMONY OF

**CELESTE DRAKE
TRADE POLICY SPECIALIST
AMERICAN FEDERATION OF LABOR &
CONGRESS OF INDUSTRIAL ORGANIZATIONS (AFL-CIO)**

DECEMBER 12, 2017

Introduction

On behalf of its 55 affiliates representing more than 12 and a half million working families, the AFL-CIO appreciates the opportunity to testify on the future of the North American Free Trade Agreement (NAFTA). The AFL-CIO represents working people in every sector of the economy, from energy and healthcare to manufacturing and retail. We provide a voice to working families, advocating for policies that will help create high quality jobs and ensure working people have the freedom to join together to negotiate for better wages and working conditions.

The AFL-CIO appreciates the Foreign Affairs Committee's interest in NAFTA renegotiation. Repeatedly, over many decades, America's workers have made recommendations for improving trade policies—only to find the bulk of our recommendations ignored. Our criticism is not against trade per se: it is about the rules governing trade. We look forward to working with Congress to advance a new set of trade rules that promote good jobs, high wages, and sustainable and responsible economic growth that protects our environment and respects human dignity.

Background: Why We Need a New NAFTA

Under NAFTA, U.S. firms and workers lost more than 850,000 jobs.[1] A much more widespread impact, though less frequently discussed, is the wage suppression that affects about two-thirds of America's workers—those who lack a college degree. As the Economic Policy Institute's Jeff Faux explains:

> "[t]he inevitable result [of NAFTA's rules] was to undercut workers' living standards all across North America. Wages and benefits have fallen behind worker productivity *in all three countries*. Moreover, despite declining wages in the United States, the gap between the typical American and typical Mexican worker in manufacturing remains the same. Even *after* adjusting for differences in living costs, Mexican workers continue to make about 30% of the wages of workers in the United States. Thus, NAFTA is both symbol and substance of the global 'race to the bottom.'"[2]

As explained at length in the AFL-CIO publication "NAFTA at 20," NAFTA and subsequent U.S. trade deals facilitate higher volumes of trade, but contain no measures to ensure that increased trade flows will be reciprocal or that any gains will be widely shared. Many of the provisions—including investor-to-state dispute settlement and limitations on banking regulations and food safety rules—actively hinder policies that would foster equitable development. While there have been modifications to NAFTA's language in subsequent agreements, the fundamental architecture that promotes broad investor rights while restricting worker freedoms and regulatory autonomy remains in place. On the whole, NAFTA-style agreements have proved to be a vehicle to

---

[1] Scott, Robert E., "The effects of NAFTA on US trade, jobs, and investment, 1993–2013," Review of Keynesian Economics, Vol. 2 No. 4, Winter 2014, pp. 429–441. *Available at:* www.elgaronline.com/view/journals/roke/2-4/roke.2014.04.02.xml.

[2] *See* Faux, Jeff, "NAFTA's Impact on U.S. Workers," EPI Working Economics Blog, Dec. 9, 2013. *Available at:* www.epi.org/blog/naftas-impact-workers/ (emphasis added).

increase corporate profits at the expense of workers, consumers, farmers, communities, the environment and even democracy itself.[3]

While one need look no further than the staunch defense of the current NAFTA by the U.S. Chamber of Commerce and the U.S. Council for International Business to know that the current version of NAFTA has benefited some sectors of the economy, one can also easily find devastation, particularly in Mexico's agricultural sector[4] and America's manufacturing heartland.[5] The paltry Trade Adjustment Assistance[6] program provides no help to working people whose wages, healthcare and retirement benefits have been pushed down by NAFTA's relentless race to the bottom, nor does it help devastated communities rebuild their tax base, build new infrastructure, or provide needed services to the un- and underemployed and those who find themselves in precarious "jobs" with uncertain incomes in the new digital economy.

Trade policy should never be a question of "free trade" versus "protectionism." The AFL-CIO's recommended frame for NAFTA renegotiation is "How should the U.S. structure international trade rules so that they promote good, family-wage jobs, sustainable growth, dynamic economies, smart natural resource conservation, and the realization of human rights and dignity globally?" We believe that using this frame will lead to better trade policy choices and better outcomes for working families.

As Josh Bivens explains in his 2017 piece *Adding Insult to Injury*, this complex frame is what has been missing from U.S. trade policy, which seems to have been based on a misunderstanding of who benefits from trade. An extended excerpt is warranted:

> "When people say that economics teaches that expanded trade is a 'win-win' proposition, this means only that trade is 'win-win' for total national income in each partner country. But textbook economics does *not* predict that expanded trade will be a win-win for all groups within those countries. . . .
>
> "Because it can be shown that the sum of capital's gains exceeds labor's losses, globalization remains "win-win" at the country level. *Within* the U.S., however, there is nothing "win-win" about it; labor loses not just in *relative* terms, but can suffer *absolute* income losses as well.
>
> "Importantly, these losses are not the damage stemming from the adjustment cost of manufacturing workers' temporary unemployment spell[s] . . . . Rather, the big

---

[3] For more detail, see "NAFTA at 20," AFL-CIO Report, March 2014. *Available at:* https://aflcio.org/reports/nafta-20.

[4] *See. e.g.*, Wise, Timothy, Agricultural Dumping Under NAFTA: Estimating the Costs of U.S. Agricultural Policies to Mexican Producers, Global Development and Environment Institute Working Paper No. 09-08, Tufts University, December 2009. *Available at:* http://www.ase.tufts.edu/gdae/Pubs/wp/09-08AgricDumping.pdf.

[5] *See, e.g.*, Stockman, Farah, "Becoming a Steelworker Liberated Her. Then Her Job Moved to Mexico," The New York Times, Oct. 14, 2017. *Available at:* https://www.nytimes.com/2017/10/14/us/union-jobs-mexico-rexnord.html.

[6] *See, e.g.*, DePillis, Lydia, "Obama's proposal to help workers who lose out on trade deals probably won't win Democratic votes." *The Washington Post*, Feb. 3, 2015. *Available at:* https://www.washingtonpost.com/news/wonk/wp/2015/02/03/obamas-proposal-to-help-workers-who-lose-out-on-trade-deals-probably-wont-win-democratic-votes/?utm_term=.84089ecc8fb8.

damage is the *permanent* wage loss resulting from America's new pattern of specialization that requires less labor and more capital. Further, this wage loss is not just suffered by workers in tradeable goods sectors who are displaced by imports; it's suffered by *all* workers who resemble these workers in terms of credentials and labor market characteristics. A simple way to say this is that while landscapers may not be displaced by imports, their wages suffer from having to compete with apparel (and auto, and steel) workers who have been displaced by imports."[7]

The following charts show the impact of this model of trade—and other neoliberal economic policies—on U.S. wages and the share of U.S. national income going to working people.

Figure 1: Gap Between U.S. Worker Productivity and Wages Is Growing

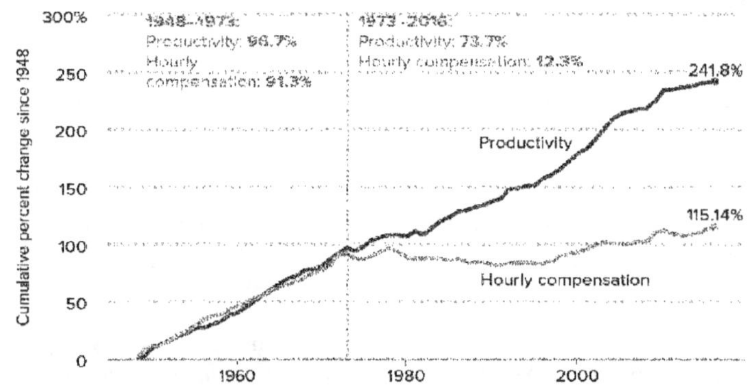

Note: Data are for compensation (wages and benefits) of production/nonsupervisory workers in the private sector and net productivity of the total economy. "Net productivity" is the growth of output of goods and services less depreciation per hour worked.

Source: EPI analysis of Bureau of Labor Statistics and Bureau of Economic Analysis data

Updated from Figure A in *Raising America's Pay: Why It's Our Central Economic Policy Challenge*

Economic Policy Institute

---

[7] Bivens, Josh, "Adding Insult to Injury: How bad policy decisions have amplified globalization's costs for American workers," Economic Policy Institute, Jul. 11, 2017. *Available at:* http://www.epi.org/publication/adding-insult-to-injury-how-bad-policy-decisions-have-amplified-globalizations-costs-for-american-workers/.

Figure 2: Workers' Share of National Income is Shrinking

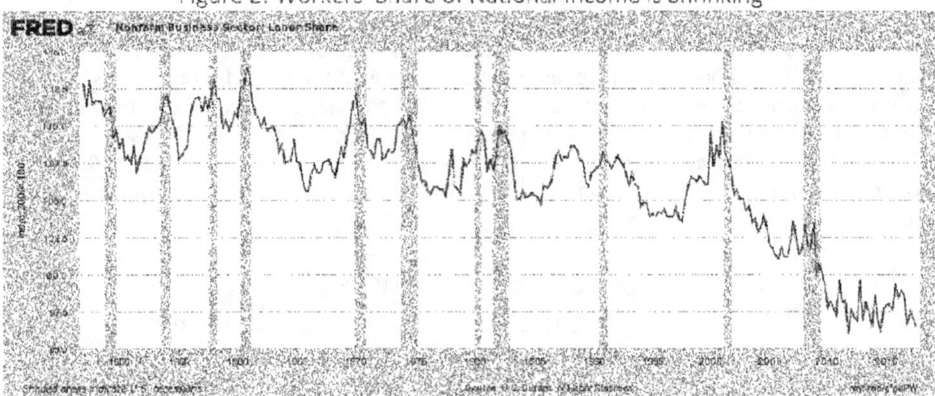

Source: Created with the FRED Economic Data Tool of the St. Louis Federal Reserve Bank. Available at: https://fred.stlouisfed.org/ (Dec. 8, 2017).

As these graphs demonstrate, even if the size of the U.S. economic pie is growing, if the rules governing our economy are not carefully crafted, the bulk of the population gets a smaller slice, as is happening currently. Although it is important to note that trade policy is not the sole cause of the trends examined here, it is an important one, in particular because it takes more than a single act of Congress or a single Executive Order to change the rules enshrined in NAFTA or any other trade agreement. It takes the consent of all parties involved.

Protectionism is not the answer, but changing the rules of trade is. To make any new NAFTA successful, the administration and Congress must ensure that a new trade deal incorporates different incentives. In other words, the structure of the new NAFTA must recognize that current trade and globalization rules have pushed wages down and weakened worker negotiating power. It must build in counterbalancing incentives and tools to raise wages, empower working people, protect precious natural resources, and address the United States' persistent trade deficit. In addition, in conjunction with the deal itself, Congress should enact a broad set of domestic industrial and economic policies to rebuild, repair and modernize U.S. infrastructure; support research, development and advanced manufacturing; and provide working people with state of the art education and skills. Absent these investments, a new NAFTA seems poised to continue to leave workers behind.

We also caution against viewing NAFTA renegotiation as an effective growth strategy in and of itself. Given the already low levels of tariffs worldwide, the opportunities for large efficiency gains due to trade are largely exhausted.[8] We should improve NAFTA because NAFTA needs

---

[8] *See, e.g.*, Krugman, Paul, "A Protectionist Moment?," The Conscience of a Liberal (Column), *The New York Times*, Mar. 9, 2016. *Available at*: https://krugman.blogs.nytimes.com/2016/03/09/a-protectionist-moment/; Amiti, Mary and Mandel, Benjamin, "Will the United States Benefit from the Trans-Pacific Partnership?," Liberty Street Economics Blog, Federal Reserve Bank of New York, May 16, 2014. *Available at*: http://libertystreeteconomics.newyorkfed.org/2014/05/will-the-united-states-benefit-from-the-trans-pacific-partnership.html#.Vr4TO_krLcy.

improving—not as a substitute for a purposeful growth policy. For example, the U.S. could achieve far greater growth, far faster, by investing in our own economy. As the International Monetary Fund has demonstrated, an infrastructure investment of 1% of GDP will result in an increase in GDP of almost 3% a mere four years after the investment.[9] This outcome is six times the projected outcome of the failed Trans-Pacific Partnership and would occur more than four times more quickly. In addition, according to economic modeling results by Ozlem Onaran of the University of Greenwich for the L20 in 2014, the U.S. could achieve as much as **9.84% growth over five years** by coordinating a 1% of GDP infrastructure investment with wage-led growth policies.[10]

A New NAFTA That Meets the Needs of Working People Will Respond to the Popular Backlash Against the Current Form of Globalization

Working people who advocate for better trade policies often face the simplistic response "Globalization is here to stay. You can't cut the U.S. off from the rest of the world, so just get over it." This response misrepresents the problem and misunderstands the proposed solution.

Unions, faith communities, health advocates, environmental organizations, migrants rights organizations and small farmers and ranchers who complain of the harmful effects of NAFTA and other trade arrangements (such as the World Trade Organization) do not advocate building walls or turning back the clock. In fact, many working people and their employers rely on exports for some or all of their income. Reformers simply want to change the rules under which trade and globalization operate. Throwing up ones hands and saying that low wages, skyrocketing drug prices, dangerous imports and environmental crimes are inevitable is not only wrong, it is counterproductive.

Globalization was shaped by the rules of NAFTA and the WTO, and it can be reshaped by alternative rules. Such reshaping is necessary if the U.S. and its allies are interested in more, rather than fewer trade arrangements—and outcome that appears to be in doubt given the United Kingdom's impending exit from the European Union, the United States exit from the Trans-Pacific Partnership, and the stalled negotiations on a number of other agreements, including the Trans-Atlantic Trade and Investment Partnership.

---

[9] "Chapter 3: Is It Time for an Infrastructure Push? The Macroeconomic Effects of Public Investment," in World Economic Outlook, International Monetary Fund, Oct. 2014. *Available at*: https://www.imf.org/external/pubs/ft/weo/2014/02/pdf/c3.pdf. See especially p. 83 ("[A] debt-financed public investment shock of 1 percentage point of GDP increases the level of output by about 0.9 percent in the same year and by 2.9 percent four years after the shock . . ."); Larry Summers, "Why public investment really is a free lunch: The IMF finds that a dollar of spending increases output by nearly $3," Larry Summers Blog, Oct. 7, 2014. *Available at*: http://larrysummers.com/2014/10/07/why-public-investment-really-is-a-free-lunch/#sthash.5fkH0nJ6.dpuf.

[10] Ozlem Onaran, "The Case for a Coordinated Policy Mix of Wage-led Recovery and Public Investment in the G20, L20 in partnership with ITUC, TUAC, and the Council of Global Unions, Jun. 2014. Available at: http://www.ituc-csi.org/IMG/pdf/modeling.pdf

As Harvard economist Dani Rodrik writes, trade breeds opposition when it "violates norms embodied in our institutional arrangements."[11] In other words, trade arrangements become unpopular not just when they affect jobs, but when they undermine hard fought protections such as the right to join together in unions to negotiate for better. Rodrik continues:

> "The benefit of thinking about fair trade along these lines is that it allows the drawing of a clear line between trade flows that threaten legitimate domestic political arrangements and those that don't. For example, there is a clear distinction between situations where a trade partner's low wages are due to low productivity, and the abuse of worker rights (including, say, the absence of collective bargaining, or freedom of association). Both may generate distributional implications at home, but there is a problem of unfair trade only in the second case."[12]

Similarly, Nobel Prize winning economist Joseph Stiglitz has written recently about the growing opposition to globalization in both developed and developing countries. How can it be that the ordinary citizens of both the developed and developing worlds see the current trade and globalization regime as harmful? Stiglitz explains that the common dissatisfaction is a result of rigged rules that "weaken workers' bargaining power. What corporations wanted was cheaper labor, however they could get it."[13] He notes that unless most workers view trade and globalization as benefiting them, it cannot be sustained.

This is the current dilemma. Can and will NAFTA be reformed in ways that satisfy and benefit the many instead of the few in the U.S., Canada and Mexico? If it will not, it seems likely that the social fabric in each country will continue to deteriorate and harmful populist rhetoric will increase, as families become more dissatisfied and angry about broken promises by governments that do the bidding of economic elites while ignoring the common good.[14]

Raising Wages and Ensuring High Labor Standards Are Step One

By putting the U.S., Canada, and Mexico into competition for investment without ensuring that each country not only had high standards on paper but an effective enforcement regime for worker and environmental protections, NAFTA acted as an anchor, dragging down tax revenues, wages and environmental standards, not just in the U.S., but in all three NAFTA countries. Because of the incentives imposed by NAFTA and similar trade policies, income distributions

---

[11] Rodrik, Dani, "It's Time to Think for Yourself on Free Trade: What economists and populists both get wrong about the international economy," Foreign Policy, Jan. 27, 2017. *Available at*: http://foreignpolicy.com/2017/01/27/its-time-to-think-for-yourself-on-free-trade/.

[12] *Id.*

[13] Stiglitz, Joseph, "Globalisation: time to look at historic mistakes to plot the future," *The Guardian*, Dec. 5, 2017. *Available at*: https://www.theguardian.com/business/2017/dec/05/globalisation-time-look-at-past-plot-the-future-joseph-stiglitz.

[14] Dolan, Eric, "'Oligarchic tendencies': Study finds only the wealthy get represented in the Senate," Raw Story, Aug. 19, 2013. *Available at*: https://www.rawstory.com/2013/08/oligarchic-tendencies-study-finds-only-the-wealthy-get-represented-in-the-senate/.

became more unequal as global companies captured an ever-larger share and workers an ever-smaller share.[15]

All the NAFTA renegotiation efforts in the world will not create U.S. jobs, raise U.S. wages, or reduce the U.S. trade deficit if the new rules do not include clear, strong, and effective labor rules that require Mexico to abandon its low wage policy[16] and instead implement and enforce the fundamental labor rights developed by businesses, working people and governments at the International Labor Organization. The pull factor of poverty wages, denial of worker freedoms, and exploitive working conditions simply cannot be counterbalanced by new rules of origin or digital trade rules alone. Working families and their advocates across North America are united in their support for greater workplace protections, a level playing field, and higher wages.

With few exceptions, Mexican "unions" are undemocratic and aligned more with employers or local political elites than with workers. These employer-dominated unions often sign contracts without any participation or input from workers for the sole purpose of interfering with the right to form effective, worker-directed unions. The government has gone along with this practice as part of a low-wage development strategy. The cumulative effect of these bogus unions is to lower wages and working conditions in Mexico.[17] Improving wages will reduce the ability of employers to use NAFTA as a tool of arbitrage that pushes wages down across North America. Higher wages in Mexico not only are good for Mexico's working families, they are a required outcome of beneficial trade policy. Raising wages in Mexico must be one of the most important outcomes of NAFTA renegotiation, or the effort will not affect outsourcing, trade balances or wage stagnation.

When workers lack the freedom to speak up about workplace conditions and negotiate together to improve their lives and livelihoods, wages, benefits and job safety are lower than they would otherwise be. NAFTA's race to the bottom has led to a global weakness in demand that hampers gross domestic product (GDP) growth and exacerbates inequality. Even the IMF has recognized a link between the decline in unionization and the dramatic increase in inequality worldwide.[18]

Those who advocate to maintain trade policies that drive wages ever lower in the relentless pursuit of quarterly profits and "competitiveness" ignore the fact that workers also are consumers. Consumers drive the demand necessary to support the global economy. This one-sided vision of competitiveness has limited the potential for U.S. exports. Indeed, wage suppression in Mexico means that there are even more Mexicans living in poverty than before

---

[15] *See* Capaldo, Jeronim et al., "Trading Down: Unemployment, Inequality and Other Risks of the Trans-Pacific Partnership Agreement," Global Development and Environment Institute Working Paper No. 16–01, January 2016, at pp. 12–13. *Available at:* www.ase.tufts.edu/gdae/Pubs/wp/16-01Capaldo-IzurietaTPP.pdf.
[16] *See, e.g.,* U.S. Rep. Sandy Levin, Press Release: NAFTA's Top Problem: Mexico's Industrial Policy of Low Wages and No Rights, Oct. 10, 2017. *Available at:* https://levin.house.gov/press-release/naftas-top-problem-mexicos-industrial-policy-low-wages-and-no-rights.
[17] *See* NAFTA at 20, *supra* note 3.
[18] Jaumotte, Florence, and Buitron, Carolina Osorio, "Power from the People," Finance & Development, Vol. 52, No. 1, International Monetary Fund, March 2015. *Available at:* www.imf.org/external/pubs/ft/fandd/2015/03/jaumotte.htm.

NAFTA,[19] that immigration push-factors have not abated, and that Mexico has become an increasingly attractive investment target.

It is too early to judge the NAFTA renegotiations a success or failure. To date, it is not clear whether any of the negotiating parties have taken our advice. While some interesting and potentially beneficial proposals have been made (including Canada's proposal to expand workplace freedoms and worker protections and the U.S. proposals to radically restrict investor-to-state dispute settlement and to incorporate a periodic review mechanism to measure whether NAFTA is achieving results), many other proposals fall in the category of "trade policy as usual" or worse, would radically expand the privileges granted to global banks and brand name pharmaceutical companies.

Recommendations[20]

The AFL-CIO's NAFTA recommendations (included below in summary form) are comprehensive, and include changes not just to the labor provisions, but to most chapters of NAFTA, as well as to domestic policies. The 2016 elections showed that America's working people are not satisfied with the status quo. They have heard promises about the benefits of trade—but seen those benefits accrue to global corporations and economic elites. It is imperative that Congress provide a comprehensive response that improves trade and related policies. NAFTA renegotiation cannot be just mere tweaks or the importation of rules from the failed TPP. Working people are ready to support beneficial changes to NAFTA. We will oppose any NAFTA that continues the status quo, even if it carries a "new and improved" label.

1. Democratize the Renegotiation Process

The TPP negotiations demonstrated that secrecy breeds contempt. NAFTA renegotiation must be transparent, democratic and participatory, with more access for Congress and the public to proposals and negotiating texts. There must be opportunities for public comment, periodic congressional hearings to review progress and more inclusive trade advisory committees.

2. Add Strong Labor Rules with Swift and Certain Enforcement

To help raise wages and improve working conditions, NAFTA must ensure all working people can exercise the fundamental labor rights reflected in International Labor Organization (ILO) labor conventions, including the bedrock right to form unions and bargain collectively. NAFTA must embed strong labor obligations in the text and establish an independent enforcement mechanism with innovative tools and penalties to overcome entrenched indifference and hostility to worker rights, including the use of violence in Mexico. The new provisions must ensure that labor reforms are measured by performance, not merely changes on paper, and they must address the failed labor case against Guatemala, which provided strong evidence that the existing

---

[19] Weisbrot, Mark, et al., "Did NAFTA Help Mexico? An Update After 23 Years," Center for Economic and Policy Research, updated March 2017. *Available at*: http://cepr.net/images/stories/reports/nafta-mexico-update-2017-03.pdf?v=2.

[20] For an expanded explanation of the AFL-CIO's NAFTA renegotiation recommendations, please see our submission to the U.S. Trade Policy Staff Committee, "How to Make NAFTA Work for Working People," available at: https://aflcio.org/statements/written-comments-how-make-nafta-work-working-people.

framework is not only ineffective, but wholly inadequate, setting up barriers to effective enforcement of trade obligations.

3. Eliminate Investor-to-State Dispute Settlement and Minimum Standard of Treatment

Investor-to-state dispute settlement (ISDS) is a separate justice system for foreign investors. It discriminates against U.S.-located firms by providing extraordinary procedural and substantive rights to foreign-based investors. According to the Cato Institute, "It is effectively a subsidy that mitigates risk for U.S. multinational corporations and enables foreign MNCs [multinational corporations] to circumvent U.S. courts when lodging complaints about U.S. policies."[21] By offering additional legal protections beyond those that exist under U.S. law or other countries' national courts, ISDS makes it more attractive to send production and investment overseas.

As one of the lawyers who brought a case against the United States on behalf of a Canadian company explained, "[The ISDS provision in] NAFTA does clearly create some rights for foreign investors that local citizens and companies don't have. But that's the whole purpose of it."[22] Rule of law requires that the law—including the system of justice—apply to everyone equally. ISDS violates this bedrock principle of democracy. ISDS also disadvantages U.S. companies that only produce in the United States (e.g., micro- and small- to medium-sized companies) because they have fewer rights than their foreign-owned competitors.

Eliminating ISDS will protect democracy, Article III of the Constitution and America's rich jurisprudence while eliminating a subsidy to companies that choose to produce abroad. Moreover, the new NAFTA must abolish the vague and overbroad "minimum standard of treatment" (MST) obligation that goes far beyond the property rights available under the U.S. Constitution.[23]

4. Create Jobs by Adding Enforceable Currency Rules

NAFTA must include enforceable currency disciplines subject to trade sanctions in the text of the agreement.[24] NAFTA parties should also commit to coordinating enforcement efforts with respect to the currency manipulation and misalignment by non-NAFTA countries. The goal of both provisions would be to reduce the unsustainable U.S. trade deficit by addressing issues of

---

[21] Ikenson, Daniel J., "A Compromise to Advance the Trade Agenda: Purge Negotiations of Investor-State Dispute Settlement," Cato Institute's Free Trade Bulletin No. 57, March 4, 2014. *Available at:* www.cato.org/publications/free-trade-bulletin/compromise-advance-trade-agenda-purge-negotiations-investor-state.
[22] Greider, William, "The Right and US Trade Law: Invalidating the 20th Century: How the right is using trade law to overturn American democracy," The Nation, Nov. 17, 2001. *Available at:* www.thenation.com/article/right-and-us-trade-law-invalidating-20th-century#.
[23] Even the staunchly free trade Cato Institute's Simon Lester calls the minimum standard of treatment a "poorly written" provision. Lester, Simon, "Responding to the White House Response on ISDS," Cato at Liberty Blog, Feb. 27, 2015. *Available at:* www.cato.org/blog/responding-white-house-defense-investor-state-dispute-settlement.
[24] There are many ways to establish such enforceable provisions against currency manipulation and misalignment. During the TPP negotiations, for example, two useful proposals included a test promoted by the American Automotive Policy Council and the incorporation of the International Monetary Fund's seven factor guidelines.

trade and exchange rates. Currency realignment would create 2.3 million to 5.8 million jobs over the next three years.[25]

5. Strengthen Rules of Origin

In general, "rules of origin" should be set so that domestic producers and workers in the NAFTA signatory countries are the primary beneficiaries of NAFTA, not third-party countries that take on no trade obligations. Strengthening the auto regional value content and closing related loopholes is important, but is not the only way to address this recommendation. The parties must also strengthen content requirements for steel, aluminum, textiles and apparel, and aerospace products, for example. Strong rules of origin will provide an incentive to produce in North America as opposed to China, Vietnam or other export platforms that exploit workers, and the incorporation of labor and other reforms suggested elsewhere in this document will ensure workers in *all three* NAFTA countries can benefit.

6. Protect Responsible Government Purchasing and Buy American Policies

NAFTA should support domestic job creation efforts by eliminating procurement commitments and promoting responsible bidding standards.[26] Currently, NAFTA gives bidders from all NAFTA countries expansive access to U.S. goods, services and construction contracts. These provisions can undermine not only domestic preferences, but also responsible bidding criteria (such as requirements that a bidder have no outstanding environmental cleanup obligations or the implementation of a system that awards bonus points for bidders with better safety records or that source from local farms). Arbitrary procurement commitments curtail efforts to ensure bidders—from any NAFTA Party—are not unfairly undercut by unscrupulous employers, which is a further reason to eliminate procurement commitments.

The United States' trade obligations open far more U.S. procurement (by dollar amount and by percentage) to foreign bidders than any other large economy.[27] Instead of blindly repeating existing procurement rules, NAFTA Parties should work to develop transparent, multilingual bidding systems and responsible employer standards that will benefit enterprises and workers located within North America, while leaving our democracies the freedom to choose when domestic preferences are necessary and appropriate, and when other considerations should prevail. The new rules should continue the prohibition on government offsets.

---

[25] Scott, Robert E., "Stop Currency Manipulation and Create Millions of Jobs, With Gains across States and Congressional Districts," EPI Briefing Paper #372, Economic Policy Institute, Feb. 26, 2014. *Available at:* www.epi.org/publication/stop-currency-manipulation-and-create-millions-of-jobs/

[26] Although there is room for additional study of the impacts of existing procurement deals (e.g., an analysis of the job and wage effects of the reciprocal agreement between the United States and Canada that was adopted for the expenditure of American Recovery and Reinvestment Act funds and an analysis of U.S. procurement contracts won by multinational versus domestic-only firms), to date, there is simply no evidence to suggest that the current procurement rules create U.S. jobs or raise U.S. wages.

[27] U.S. Government Accountability Office, "Government Procurement: United States Reported Opening More Opportunities to Foreign Firms than Other Countries, but Better Data Are Needed," February 2017, Fig. 2, p. 12. *Available at:* www.gao.gov/products/GAO-17-168.

7. Eliminate Chapter 19 Obstacles to Effective Trade Enforcement

Chapter 19 should be eliminated and replaced with a mechanism for North American cooperation to ensure effective enforcement against unfairly traded products from non-NAFTA countries

8. Combat Tax Dodging

NAFTA and subsequent trade and globalization rules have had a negative long-term impact on tax revenues and public investment. In addition, through a variety of legal and illegal tax avoidance schemes, tax revenues have fallen for jurisdictions around the world, regardless of tax rates. This troubling trend undermines the social contract and inhibits robust public investment in infrastructure and human capital. The new NAFTA should address base erosion and tax avoidance to help meet infrastructure needs and cultivate public support for international trade. If trade rules are beneficial, they should help America build new schools, high-speed communications networks, and transportation corridors. But if trade is viewed as a vehicle to facilitate tax dodging by economic elites, public opposition will only grow.

9. Remove Rules That Undermine Protections for Workers, Consumers and the Environment

NAFTA must not limit, undermine or inhibit public interest standards or regulations. NAFTA must ensure that North America's democracies retain the freedom to develop, advance and implement commonsense protections, including country-of-origin labeling, free from the threat of trade challenges. The renegotiated NAFTA must contain no negative lists, no ratchet clauses and no "regulatory impact analysis" requirements. Negative list commitments in NAFTA must be rewritten into positive list commitments to ensure that North American democracies retain to right to advance commonsense rules relevant to newly developed services, free from the threat of trade challenges.

While the AFL-CIO agrees that, under the right circumstances, regulatory cooperation can increase trade and efficiency in ways that benefit workers and consumers, we also caution against blunt efforts to use NAFTA renegotiation as a back-door route to attack important worker, consumer, environmental, health and food safety protections. Deregulation via international negotiations is inherently undemocratic, reducing trust in both trade and democracy because it undermines standards that citizens struggled to enact (such as "COOL" labeling).

10. Add Commitments to Invest in Infrastructure

Investing in infrastructure drives long-term, broadly shared growth, but is hard to do when global companies are driving a race to the bottom. Adding an infrastructure commitment will help offset the incentives of prior trade deals that have depressed public investment.

Specifically, NAFTA must include a new chapter in which each Party commits itself to investing a minimum of 3% of its GDP annually in its own public infrastructure construction, repair and maintenance. The commitment must ensure that preferences for domestic procurement are allowable. Parties shall determine their respective infrastructure priorities with public input, and all public construction, repair and maintenance investments (transit, aviation, bridges, roads, ports, water, sewer, electricity, communications, schools, parks, other public facilities, etc.) shall count toward the minimum. The idea behind this provision is simple: set a reasonable target[28] for public infrastructure spending and require Parties to report their actual spending annually. The public reporting aspect will assist local, state and federal policy makers in evaluating their respective investments and helping their economies to grow.

Separately, and in addition, the NAFTA implementing bill must contain one-time mandatory funding for specific trade-related projects in the United States, to enhance the benefits working families can reap from North American trade, including but not limited to new and improved land border crossings; ports, airports, roadways and waterways; new and improved rail corridors, including high-speed rail; and broadband infrastructure, including in rural communities.

11. Protect Consumers and Ensure Financial Stability

A new NAFTA should not expand financial services commitments or limit regulation of the financial sector. NAFTA should protect the ability to engage in fair and nondiscriminatory application of capital controls and other measures to ensure the stability of the financial system. As Philip R. Lane explains in his paper, "Financial Globalization and the Crisis," financial globalization enabled the scaling-up of the U.S. "securitization boom" that triggered the crisis and was a key factor in the rise of large credit growth differences and current account imbalances that propelled the crisis across countries.[29] NAFTA Parties must incorporate the lessons learned from the aggressive financial deregulation of the 1990s and resist the entreaties of Wall Street and Canadian banks to use NAFTA renegotiation to ease financial services regulation.

12. Promote Transportation Safety

The new NAFTA must ensure that all Parties may enforce domestic highway safety, labor protections and environmental standards on foreign trucks, rail and buses. In addition, NAFTA should continue its existing policy of broadly excluding water and air transportation services from coverage. This includes maintaining existing reservations covering the Jones Act, laws respecting ownership and control of airlines, and the like.

13. Protect Intellectual Property While Ensuring the Right to Affordable Medicines

For copyright: NAFTA should retain strong provisions to protect creative and innovative workers (including actors, writers, musicians and others) whose income, standard of living, and health and retirement benefits rely upon residuals, royalties and other payments tied to international copyright protection.

For patents and related protections: NAFTA must balance innovation with affordability of healthcare. The administration must work to ensure NAFTA's patent provisions do not become a corporate welfare program for brand-name pharmaceutical and medical device companies. Nor should NAFTA undermine democratic choices about how to ensure prescription drugs and medical devices provided through public programs are affordable for taxpayers and beneficiaries.

---

[28] According to the Congressional Budget Office, public spending on transportation and water infrastructure alone "over the past three decades has hovered at about 2.4 percent," "Public Spending on Transportation and Water Infrastructure, 1956 to 2014," CBO, March 2015. *Available at:* www.cbo.gov/sites/default/files/114th-congress-2015-2016/reports/49910-Infrastructure.pdf.

[29] Lane, Philip R., "Financial Globalisation and the Crisis," Prepared for the 11th BIS Annual Conference on The Future of Financial Globalisation, Lucerne, Jun. 21–22, 2012.

Reproducing TPP provisions on patents, exclusivity and so-called "transparency and procedural fairness" into a renegotiated NAFTA would be a step backward for the health of working families in the United States, Canada and Mexico, and is unacceptable.

14. Prohibit Global Corporations from Using NAFTA to Capture Public Services for Profit

NAFTA renegotiation must expand the public services exception so that public services are fully carved out, or protected, from the agreement. The current NAFTA text leaves out a number of important public services, including energy, postal, water and sewer, sanitation, immigration and public transportation services from its Annex II reservation. This shortcoming must be rectified to protect the full spectrum of democratic decision making regarding the provision of public services.

15. Add Strong Environmental Rules with Swift and Certain Enforcement

NAFTA must be reformed to include strong environmental standards that will be enforced. NAFTA must require adoption of and compliance with key multilateral environmental agreements; prohibit illegal trade of timber and wildlife; promote responsible fisheries; and ensure countries cannot gain an unfair trade advantage by allowing highly polluting practices. This should be done in a manner akin to the recommendations for labor obligations.

16. Improve Screening for Foreign Direct Investment

Congress and the administration should work together to enhance the powers of the Committee on Foreign Investment in the United States to be sure the U.S. can review greenfield investments and use a "net economic benefit test" to measure more impacts on our working people as a whole. In addition, NAFTA should be updated to accommodate this domestic policy change.

17. Improve Trade Enforcement as Part of a Robust Manufacturing Policy

Trade rules are only as good as their enforcement. Enforcement tools must be expanded and used promptly. Rules crafted to create a fair and level playing field and promote good jobs in growing industries will support employment and wage growth in all three NAFTA countries. This will be a significant improvement over the current rules, which reward low-road practices, harming businesses, farms and working families across North America.

18. Improve the ITC's Economic Modeling

The United States International Trade Commission (ITC) is responsible for projecting the economic outcomes of proposed U.S. trade and investment negotiations. The ITC uses a model called the computable general equilibrium (CGE). The CGE has a number of limitations and does not adequately address such issues as mercantilist trade policies, currency manipulation, long-term wage stagnation or inefficiencies that result from trade deal-caused deregulation, privatization, market concentration or deunionization. As a result, the ITC's past projections been *over* rather than *under* optimistic.[30] Importantly, the CGE method is particularly ill suited to NAFTA renegotiations, as tariffs for nearly all traded goods already are at zero.

---

[30] *See, e.g.*, Drake, Celeste, on behalf of the AFL-CIO, Oral Testimony on "Investigation No. TPA-105-001, Trans-Pacific Partnership Agreement: Likely Impact on the U.S. Economy and on Specific Industry Sectors," Before the U.S. International Trade Commission, Jan. 13, 2016. *Available at:* www.usitc.gov/press_room/documents/testimony/105_001_005.pdf.

Mr. Poe. Thank you.

Thank all of you.

I will recognize myself for 5 minutes.

Just answer this question "yes" or "no"; it is easy. Has NAFTA benefited the United States?

Mr. Farnsworth?

Mr. Farnsworth. Yes.

Mr. Poe. Mr. Allford?

Mr. Allford. Yes.

Mr. Poe. And Ambassador?

Mr. Negroponte. Yes.

Mr. Poe. Ms. Drake?

Ms. Drake. No.

Mr. Poe. Three to one.

Mr. Allford, you heard the testimony of Ms. Drake. And you started out as a single owner, inventor, businessperson, worker. You were all of the above when you started. You said NAFTA has helped you. You have 65 employees. Is that correct?

Mr. Allford. That is correct.

Mr. Poe. How much of your trade—how much do you trade with Mexico? Can you give us a percentage?

Mr. Allford. Over the last 3 years, it has been 15 percent of our revenues, but it fluctuates year to year.

Mr. Poe. Okay. How about Canada?

Mr. Allford. Again, the same, 15 percent.

Mr. Poe. What would happen to your business if the United States hit the road with NAFTA?

Mr. Allford. We would probably lay off 15 people.

Mr. Poe. Ambassador, the renegotiation with NAFTA is taking place now. What should we do, the United States do, to make it better, specifically?

Mr. Negroponte. Well, I think some of the changes, the new concepts that were introduced to the Trans-Pacific Partnership, which, of course, we have not entered into—we have withdrawn from that agreement. But in that TPP negotiation, things like intellectual property protection, e-commerce, updating the labor and environmental provisions, those kinds of features are things that I believe ought to also be introduced into a bilateral—or into the NAFTA discussion.

And my understanding is that they have been, although, like Ms. Drake, I haven't seen the specific language being discussed, but——

Mr. Poe. So you agree with her that we need to update the labor provisions in NAFTA?

Mr. Negroponte. Yes. And I——

Mr. Poe. For the United States. That would benefit the United States.

Mr. Negroponte. Right. And just as a reminder of the history of this, I think we have to remember that in 1993 and 1994 the labor and environmental provisions were sort of an afterthought. In other words, Mr. Bush signed the agreement, and then Mr. Clinton, as a condition, when he came into office, for actually going through with the agreement, insisted on negotiating these environmental and labor accords. And so it really was an afterthought. I think now it is less so.

Mr. POE. Mr. Farnsworth, I mentioned in my opening statement that United States policy, economic policy, foreign policy, whatever you want to call it, we seem to get involved in working with countries across the seas and trying to help their economy, but we seem to ignore our neighbors, specifically helping the economy of Mexico, which I think not only helps Mexico, it helps us.

Do you agree with that statement?

Mr. FARNSWORTH. Judge Poe, I strongly agree with that statement, and I thank you for raising that as a priority of this hearing.

Mexico also has politics, and Mexicans will go to the polls in July for a Presidential election. It is too early, at this point, to declare who is going to be the winner in Mexico, but simply to say that, to the extent they feel that the United States is being a partner that is looking to distance the relationship rather than make it closer, that could very well encourage folks to vote for candidates in the Mexican process who may take a view of the United States that is less charitable.

And the last thing we would want, in my view, would be to have a Mexico that views the United States in the way that we had in terms of the relationship back before NAFTA was finalized.

We have to remember that the recent relationship over the last 23, 24 years is actually not the traditional relationship that Mexico and the United States have had. That relationship tended to be more acrimonious at times, but, at the best of times, benign.

Now, over the last 23, 24 years, we have had the opportunity for real, intensive, and mutually supportive cooperation across a range of issues, yes, on the economy but also on the security side and on the migration side, and that would be put immediately at risk. Mexico has its own interests; they might view some of these issues differently. And I think we have to remember that.

Mr. POE. Historically, the relationship between Mexico and the United States, especially Mexico and Texas, has been tense, in my opinion, and has changed for the better but slowly. I think we need to work with our next-door neighbors and look at them closer than we start—people across the seas.

And one last question. Does Mexico and Canada want to renegotiate NAFTA? Anybody can weigh on this. Just "yes" or "no."

Mr. FARNSWORTH. Yes, they have indicated a willingness to do so.

Mr. POE. Ambassador, I think you wanted to say something?

Mr. NEGROPONTE. Yes, sir. I think they do, but within limits. I think there are some provisions that have been suggested that I think they probably would not be willing to accept. For example, a sunset provision, a 5-year sunset provision, would be one, I think, rather significant example of——

Mr. POE. A sunset provision is bad for business, wouldn't you think?

Mr. NEGROPONTE. Well, it is hard to make an investment——

Mr. POE. That is right.

Mr. NEGROPONTE [continuing]. If you only have 5 years.

Mr. POE. I will yield to the ranking member, Mr. Keating from Massachusetts.

Mr. KEATING. Thank you, Mr. Chairman.

And, indeed, a lot has happened over the last decades since the NAFTA agreement was negotiated. One of those areas is really—and I mentioned the growth of Mr. Allford's business is indicating that—the growth of artificial intelligence and robotics and the new industries there.

So I would like to ask you all, you know, given that, you know, what importance in retraining workers and preparing them for new industries should be part of this agreement in terms of promoting this? You know, can we use this opportunity to deal with, you know, the dislocation that comes from these new industries? Can we use this to make sure that American workers have the option of retraining and have the resources to do it, in preparing them for these new industries?

Ms. Drake?

Ms. DRAKE. Thank you.

I think not only can we but we must do that.

The problem is that all the training and education in the world doesn't create one single job. So, while we are investing in training and education to get U.S. workers up to a world-class level, we also have to make the investments that will help create the jobs, so promoting innovation, investing in infrastructure, making the U.S. a more attractive place to invest.

Right now, it takes as long for a freight train to get from Los Angeles to Chicago as to just get through Chicago. And compare that to the investments, for example, that China is making in its infrastructure that makes it an attractive place to invest.

So we need to combine training and education to prepare workers and to retrain workers who have lost their jobs, but we also need to do the homework to make sure that we are creating those jobs for the trained workers to go into.

Mr. KEATING. I think, incidentally, as I have talked to business leaders and I asked them to prioritize their needs, enhancing our infrastructure is either one or two in everyone's comments. And that is one reason I am concerned, quite frankly, about this tax plan, because there is going to be no money left for that. And I believe infrastructure should be, if it is not parallel, incorporated with our plans.

You mentioned the Guatemalan case. Is there anything—and this is open to all our panelists—is there anything that we should learn from that case in terms of reshaping this agreement?

Ms. DRAKE. I will start, that the Guatemalan case, it lasted for more than 9 years. So one thing is just in terms of timeliness and delay.

But, secondly, there is no question on the world stage that Guatemala is not enforcing its laws, any laws—labor laws, criminal laws of any kind. The U.N. High Commissioner on Human Rights has an office there to deal specifically with rule-of-law issues and, in particular, freedom of association and human rights in the economic sphere. That is exactly what we are talking about.

But because the CAFTA, the Central American Free Trade Agreement, limited the way that we could enforce labor obligations—it had to be in a manner affecting trade and a sustained or recurring course of action, or inaction—the panel said the U.S. had failed to prove its case.

So what we have to do is make sure that these additional hurdles to labor enforcement aren't repeated in the NAFTA. Labor obligations should be as enforceable as every other obligation, and right now, with that language, they are not.

Mr. KEATING. Yeah.

I think a final question—and the panel can answer the previous question or this, as they see fit. But looking at changes that have occurred over this time and what we should take into consideration, do you think there should be commitments about climate change as part of the NAFTA or trade agreement negotiations? And why or why not?

Ms. DRAKE. I would say absolutely. And the reason why is we would not want to lose high-value manufacturing, in particular, to a trading partner that says, "Pollute all you want. Contribute to global warming all you want. You can produce here, and it will be cheaper." And the problem is that everyone has to live with the effects of putting that high carbon output into the global environment.

Mr. KEATING. Ambassador?

Mr. NEGROPONTE. Yeah, I think that—I took a look at the TPP language, and I would say it is good in terms of encouraging proper environmental behavior, but I don't think it goes so far as to impose enforcement within the agreement itself. I think it allows for domestic enforcement in each of the cases. But I think it goes farther than the agreement we had back in 1993, in terms of encouraging the right kind of environmental policies.

And having dealt with both Canada and Mexico on environment, I think they both want to make the environment better. I don't think there is any doubt about it. When I got to Mexico, you could barely see in front of your nose, there was so much particulate matter in the air. There was leaded gas; they hadn't gotten rid of leaded gas yet.

Mr. KEATING. I am encouraged, myself. I think that is one area where we have the three countries sharing some of these values together. And together, if we move forward on this, it will be a strong example for other agreements as we go forward. So it is great to have some common areas where we can agree.

And I want to thank you. This is a fascinating area. I am so pleased you are here.

And I yield back.

Mr. POE. I thank the gentleman from Massachusetts.

The Chair recognizes the gentleman from Florida, Mr. Mast.

Mr. MAST. Thank you, sir. I appreciate that.

You know, I only have 5 minutes, so I don't want to necessarily hear from everybody on each one of these questions, but I do generally open this up to each and every one of you, whoever champs at the bit first.

But I want to start by asking a little bit about e-commerce and some of the provisions that we should be looking at to strengthen what is going on with NAFTA and e-commerce in benefiting the United States of America.

I mean, obviously, that is always a fair thing to say. We can assume that Canada will be looking at any NAFTA 2.0 to strengthen
provisions for Canada. Mexico would be looking to do the same. I
think they rightfully fear any intrusion of products coming in from
Asia, which is probably the way most Americans feel about products that have come in from other places, even throughout our own
region.

But what do you see as things that we can do to strengthen e-
commerce through any NAFTA 2.0 for the United States of America?

Don't all start at once.

Mr. FARNSWORTH. There is one thing that we could do. We have
tried already in multiple fora, and it resides with the Government
of Mexico to make this decision, but we could change the de mini-
mus levels for package delivery from the United States to Mexico.
From an e-commerce perspective, that would have a potentially
dramatic impact.

Mr. MAST. Do you see the other players, Canada and Mexico,
being willing participants for compromise in this region?

Mr. FARNSWORTH. As I say, this has been a perennial issue between the United States and Mexico. They have indicated that they
are not ready to entertain those proposals, but I think we need to
continue pushing forward on that.

And this is an entire industry that really didn't even exist when
NAFTA was first negotiated. And I think the broader point here is
something that bears focus. You know, if you think back to, for example, the automobile that you were driving in 1993, mine had a
tape deck in it and that was about it. Now, the automobiles are lit-
erally driving themselves.

I mean, the world has changed so fundamentally, and NAFTA,
the provisions in the auto sector and every other sector that are included, actually still maintain the provisions, in large measure, of
the world as it existed in 1994, when NAFTA went into effect.

This is something that, from the updating perspective, we really
need to have a hard look at. And it can actually help the innovation agenda for all three economies. But there are some sand in the
gears, like the one that you have just referred to. I think that
would be a good place to start.

Mr. MAST. Are you pointing, to some degree, in terms of the origin of parts and the percentage that we need in, say, a U.S. automobile, 62 percent of it being made in the region, something like
that?

Mr. FARNSWORTH. Certainly, rules of origin plays into that, absolutely. And this is a very complicated issue, there is no question
about it. We have to be careful here. With the right intentions, if
we try to manage rules of origin in a way that is ultimately counterproductive from a commercial perspective, we could actually decrease production in the North American zone and force that production overseas in a way that is unhelpful to job creation in the
United States.

So this is something that is currently being negotiated among the
three parties right now. It is something the U.S. administration
has made a very high priority, and it is something that we have
to watch very carefully.

Mr. MAST. Yes, Ambassador? By all means.

Mr. NEGROPONTE. I think that, in part, what Mr. Farnsworth is referring to is the fact that our negotiators are asking for an explicit U.S. content of—I believe they are asking for 50 percent with respect to automobiles, as opposed to a North America-wide content of the 62.5 percent that you referred to.

And I think there is real concern amongst people who look at this that, if we were to insist on that, it would damage the competitiveness of vehicles made in North America. And it wouldn't have the effect, necessarily, of driving production back to the United States. I think it might be taken offshore to places like Asia and Europe.

Mr. MAST. And that is what we are looking for, is production here, jobs here. This is something that we want to see. I heard a little jab over there on taxes. I think one of the most important points we can make, even—it came from a Democrat President. John F. Kennedy talked about how paradoxical it is, the relationship between lowering taxes and increasing revenue. One of my favorite quotes that exists out there.

But in the aim of talking a little bit more about jobs, I have one more question, and that is, do you see anything within NAFTA that we could be renegotiating specifically to actually put Asia a little bit more on its heels and not have to worry about, necessarily, the loss there but actually put them on their heels and put them on the defensive?

Ms. DRAKE. I would say one of the recommendations that the AFL-CIO made was this commitment to work together as a three-party bloc to make sure that we are addressing tax avoidance so the taxes that are due are collected and able to be invested in infrastructure; commitments to invest by all three countries in infrastructure so that we can build that back up and make this an attractive place.

And, finally, something that is very important is to have all three countries work together to cooperate on enforcement when there are non-NAFTA parties doing trade cheating, dumping, subsidizing, whatever it is, to work together to cooperate on enforcement. And that would make the U.S. enforcement a lot stronger.

Mr. MAST. Very fair. Thank you.

Thank you for your time. Thank you for your answers.

Mr. POE. I thank the gentleman from Florida.

The Chair recognizes the gentlelady from Nevada, Ms. Titus.

Ms. TITUS. Well, thank you, Mr. Chairman.

Mr. Negroponte, you and Mr. Farnsworth both referenced in your comments concern that if this negotiation goes awry or if the U.S. pulls out of NAFTA that we will return to being distant neighbors with Mexico. I think you said the relationship in the past wasn't quite as copacetic as it is today.

I wonder what you both think the President's anti-Mexico rhetoric and call to build a wall and have them pay for it is doing for our relationship with Mexico and the potential negotiations. And if this fails, do you think a wall will be able to stop the millions who will suffer as a result of the economic consequences?

Mr. NEGROPONTE. Well, I think in atmospheric terms, I don't think that kind of rhetoric goes down particularly well in Mexico, and I think it contributes to a sense that the President may not regard Mexico and the Mexican people as highly as they would like.

But if you go to the core of it and talk to them about it in depth, what they really care about is the NAFTA and the trading relationship, and they want to see that renewed. And I think they are prepared to tolerate a certain amount of rhetoric provided the practical results are beneficial to them.

Ms. TITUS. And what about in this election that is coming up? You mentioned that perhaps someone less favorable to the U.S. would get elected because of some of this rhetoric.

Would you weigh in, Mr. Farnsworth?

Mr. FARNSWORTH. Yes, ma'am. And thank you for the question. And I agree with Ambassador Negroponte. It is not particularly helpful, and it stigmatizes, in some way, the relationship. And people don't necessarily appreciate that.

The one thing about—in reference to your question about the border wall, Ms. Drake referenced infrastructure within the United States, which I think is absolutely correct. I am actually from Chicago, and I can verify that traffic there is complicated. But to the extent that we are also building additional obstructions or obstacles with our border with Mexico, that is only going to make the commercial relationship that much more complicated, particularly in sectors that final production is not in one country or the other but that production actually crosses the border multiple times—for example, in the auto sector. And each time, if the border is congested or complicated, that reduces the efficiency of production, raises the cost of production, and ultimately make U.S. manufacturing less competitive.

And we have to remember that final goods that are exported from Mexico, according to the National Bureau of Economic Research, actually include some 40 percent of U.S. content.

So, as we are making that border more complicated to cross, we are actually impacting the commercial relationship in a way that I think is very, very compelling, and something we need to think hard before we do it.

Ms. TITUS. Thank you.

I would also like to ask you about tourism. I represent Las Vegas, and I co-chair the Travel and Tourism Caucus. And our greatest source of tourists are Mexico and Canada. I think half of all international visits came from those two countries—18.7 million last year from Mexico, 19.3 million from Canada. But we have seen a decrease, according to the Department of Commerce's National Travel and Tourism Office, from Mexico this past year, and some of that is tied to that same rhetoric that I mentioned.

Could you discuss how a poor renegotiation or withdrawing from NAFTA would address tourism as part of our economic interaction with these two countries? Anybody.

Mr. NEGROPONTE. Well, I think maybe in the broader sense. If the NAFTA fails and then it has negative, adverse economic consequences on Canada and Mexico—I could see a devaluation of their currency, for example, and then there would be all sorts of knock-on effects which might, over time, affect the ability of Mexicans to travel to the United States.

But visiting the U.S. is near and dear to their hearts. You know, a lot of visa applicants in those visa lines in Mexico are wanting to take their children to Disneyland, right? I mean, that is what they want to do, or go to Las Vegas or visit the other tourist highlights in the country.

Ms. TITUS. Mr. Farnsworth?

Mr. FARNSWORTH. Well, again, I think that, in the broadest sense, things that would indicate that the United States is a less welcoming environment to anybody coming to visit would, I think, depress the interest from Mexicans and others, frankly, in visiting the United States as tourists.

Ms. TITUS. Big difference in a wall and a welcome mat.

Thank you. I yield back.

Mr. POE. The Chair recognizes the gentlelady from California, Mrs. Torres.

Mrs. TORRES. Thank you, Mr. Chairman. And thank you for bringing us together to talk about such an important issue between North American countries.

I was recently in Mexico. I travel as part of the U.S.-Mexico Interparliamentary Group. It is heartbreaking to hear how offended—or how much our administration, our current President has offended our Mexican nationals and how he has negatively impacted our relationship with our closest neighbors to the south, neighbors who we depend on for our national security and great partner on this issue.

Ms. Drake, I agree with you on the labor and environmental issues. I think it is unfortunate that it was a second thought, it wasn't negotiated. And I think that this is an opportunity for us to really bring about labor issues, wages, and climate change issues, although we don't want to call it "climate change issues" anymore. I get that. "Weather pattern changes," as I refer to them.

Friday night, I had some gifts for my little grandbaby, and I was wrapping them. The toy was made here, the wrapping was made in China, but the ribbon—and I took a picture of it. It is on my social media. And I am happy for you if you follow me. The ribbon says it is made in Mexico from materials manufactured in the USA, Rancho Cucamonga, California, 91730. That is my neighboring city. And I was so proud of that that I had to tweet out that photo, because that is NAFTA.

I traveled through my district and visited 17 manufacturers that say they are dependent on NAFTA to trade with—you know, within businesses across. That means that those California workers, those California companies that are a part of the Paris Agreement, that are committed to ensuring that we have air quality that we can all be proud of for our future generations, will be denied those jobs. So, rather than abandoning, you know, an agreement that might have not benefited all of our communities in all of our States in the U.S.—as a matter of fact, some parts of Mexico are just as angry as some parts of the U.S. Southern Mexico, for example, has not benefited a single job, you know, from the NAFTA agreement. And they would say, just like some of our States would say in rural counties, it has negatively impacted them.

So how do we focus on those areas and ensure that, whether it is infrastructure—what are some of the ways that we can bring about this dialogue to an administration that is so much opposed to it?

Ms. Drake?

Ms. DRAKE. I would start by abandoning the us-versus-them rhetoric. It really isn't the United States versus Mexico versus China. And, in fact, the firms that are competing, the firms are global; the profits are global; the places where profits are booked and taxes are avoided are global. The only thing that is not global are the workers themselves and the worker rights.

So it really takes a change of our frame of how are we looking at this and how do we give businesses the right incentives to create jobs, not just in the U.S. but—of course in the U.S., but also in Mexico and in Canada, and to make sure that those are good jobs, family-wage jobs.

You know, there are millions more living in poverty in Mexico now than before NAFTA. It is not all attributable to NAFTA, but there are certain things that all three countries can do to try to make a more progressive economy and to create not just any job, not just a job that has no security, but really say, "We are going to work on this together."

And then what we are doing, if we are able to do that, in the context of NAFTA, to say we are going to also continue to trade and continue to grow the trade relationship, as Chairman Poe referenced earlier, it is good for the U.S. not just because you are raising wages there so we get a better labor market here, but you are creating new customers for U.S. exports. There are so many in Mexico right now that aren't really participating in the global economy and can't afford to buy American goods.

So how can we do all of that? And there are lots of ways, and it starts with labor rights, but there are many other investments we can make.

Mrs. TORRES. Thank you.

And I yield back.

Mr. POE. I thank the gentlelady.

The Chair recognizes Ms. Frankel from Florida.

Ms. FRANKEL. Thank you, Mr. Poe.

Thank you to our witnesses.

So I want to pick up where my colleague Mrs. Torres left off and just say I agree that we have to—when we rework this agreement, we have to improve the labor standards and also environmental standards.

I want to look at this from a little different angle, maybe more from the aspect of this committee on terrorism. That is, I have very mixed emotions when I think about this, because I want to do everything possible to improve America's economy; we also have to be concerned about our security.

And so I think when—Ms. Drake, I like your approach. It is not us against them. Because my big concern is, if we allow Mexico to go downhill, to have more economic losses, well, things are going to start to happen that we don't want to happen, which will be probably more illegal immigration, more violent drug trading, more border issues.

And so I would like to hear some comment on that from whoever would like to.

Mr. NEGROPONTE. If I could, Mr. Chairman, I would just like to say I think the cooperation on the security front with Mexico has been at an unprecedented level. I mean, some examples would of course be the fact that we have been cooperating on immigration issues, not only on our common border but also down on Mexico's border with Central America. So I think that is important. We have been, lately, doing a lot of good work on transnational crime and that kind of activity.

And perhaps one that is really politically very significant for Mexico, when I was Ambassador down there 25 years ago, Mexico wouldn't extradite criminals to the United States, and now they do it, and they do it without any difficulty whatsoever. And, to my mind, that really represents a major shift in their approach toward cooperation with our country.

Ms. FRANKEL. And I assume, from what you are saying, that if we just really walked away from NAFTA, that the border cooperation and the other cooperation might fail.

Mr. NEGROPONTE. Well, I certainly wouldn't want to wish that, nor would anybody, I don't suppose. But it might make it a little harder for them and give them a little less room for maneuver, politically, if they were working in the context of a failed NAFTA.

Ms. FRANKEL. Mr. Farnsworth, I see you—and Mr. Allford, you have both been shaking your head—and Ms. Drake. Who wants to——

Mr. FARNSWORTH. I have nothing in particular to add, other than to associate myself with Ambassador Negroponte's comments. I think that is exactly right.

And we also have to remember Mexico is not doing this cooperation necessarily to please the United States. It is doing it because it is in its own interests. And those interests will continue no matter what happens on the north side of the border.

So there will be, in my view, some continued level of cooperation. The question will be how easy it will be, how politically possible it will be, and what extent it will be. And you could paint a scenario, I think, quite easily that the next President of Mexico, whoever he or she may be, could not have the same level of political room to maneuver to cooperate with the United States. So I think that is a real risk. I wouldn't think that the cooperation would end, but I think perhaps it would become much more fraught.

Ms. FRANKEL. Ms. Drake, did you want to add to that?

Ms. DRAKE. Yes. Thank you.

I would just add that NAFTA has not been a magic bullet on this front. The noted economist and author Jeff Faux has done some really good work about how some of the campesinos who were pushed off the land after NAFTA ended up in the narcotrafficking regime.

And we also must note that rule of law continues to be a problem. A couple of years ago, 43 student teachers were kidnapped in Mexico. We still don't have a resolution of that. And just within the past couple of weeks, we had two labor activists who were assassinated in a worker strike in a mine.

So we have lots of work to do. And the U.S. could do a much better job of pushing Mexico to make sure that it protects workers and women as part of its rule-of-law issues.

Ms. FRANKEL. Thank you.

Mr. Allford?

Mr. ALLFORD. As you can tell, I believe that trade creates jobs. I ship machines overseas that allow people to build high-value-added products, not just wrapping ribbons. If everybody has a job, they are able to feed their family, the world is a more tranquil place.

Ms. FRANKEL. Thank you.

Thank you all for your response.

I yield back.

Mr. POE. I thank the gentlelady.

I want to thank all of you all, or all y'all, as we say as a plural to "y'all" in Texas, for being here today. The testimony has been excellent, and we appreciate your time and your information.

There may be questions that members of the panel may have. They will submit that through the Chair to you in writing. And then we would like a timely response, preferably before the NAFTA agreement is reached.

And, with that, the committee is adjourned.

[Whereupon, at 3:07 p.m., the subcommittee was adjourned.]

APPENDIX

———

MATERIAL SUBMITTED FOR THE RECORD

SUBCOMMITTEE HEARING NOTICE
COMMITTEE ON FOREIGN AFFAIRS
U.S. HOUSE OF REPRESENTATIVES
WASHINGTON, DC 20515-6128

Subcommittee on Terrorism, Nonproliferation, and Trade
Ted Poe (R-TX), Chairman

TO: MEMBERS OF THE COMMITTEE ON FOREIGN AFFAIRS

You are respectfully requested to attend an OPEN hearing of the Committee on Foreign Affairs, to be held by the Subcommittee on Terrorism, Nonproliferation, and Trade in Room 2172 of the Rayburn House Office Building (and available live on the Committee website at http://www.ForeignAffairs.house.gov):

DATE: Tuesday, December 12, 2017

TIME: 2:00 p.m.

SUBJECT: The Future of the North American Free Trade Agreement

WITNESSES: Mr. Eric Farnsworth
Vice President
Council of the Americas

Mr. Daniel Allford
President
ARC Specialties

The Honorable John D. Negroponte
Vice Chairman
McLarty Associates
(Former Deputy Secretary of State and Former Director of National Intelligence)

Ms. Celeste Drake
Trade and Globalization Policy Specialist
The American Federation of Labor and Congress of Industrial Organizations

By Direction of the Chairman

COMMITTEE ON FOREIGN AFFAIRS

MINUTES OF SUBCOMMITTEE ON _Terrorism, Nonproliferation, and Trade & Europe, Eurasia, and Emerging Threats_ HEARING

Day __Tuesday__ Date __12/12/2017__ Room __2172__

Starting Time __2:00pm__ Ending Time __3:07pm__

Recesses ____ (____to____)(____to____)(____to____)(____to____)(____to____)(____to____)

Presiding Member(s)

Representative Poe

Check all of the following that apply:

Open Session [✓]
Executive (closed) Session [ ]
Televised [ ]

Electronically Recorded (taped) [✓]
Stenographic Record [✓]

TITLE OF HEARING:

"The Future of the North American Free Trade Agreement"

SUBCOMMITTEE MEMBERS PRESENT:

Rep. Poe, Keating, Cook, Frankel, Perry, Titus, Zeldin, Torres, Mast, Schneider

NON-SUBCOMMITTEE MEMBERS PRESENT: _(Mark with an * if they are not members of full committee.)_

Rep. Wagner

HEARING WITNESSES: Same as meeting notice attached? Yes [✓] No [ ]
(if "no", please list below and include title, agency, department, or organization.)

STATEMENTS FOR THE RECORD: _(List any statements submitted for the record.)_

SFR submitted by Rep. Issa
IFR submitted by Rep. Issa

TIME SCHEDULED TO RECONVENE __________
or
TIME ADJOURNED __3:07pm__

Subcommittee Staff Associate

House Committee on Foreign Affairs
Terrorism, Non-proliferation, and Trade Subcommittee
"The Future of the NAFTA"

Statement for the record submitted by Mr. Issa of California:

In September 1993, I testified before the House Ways & Means Committee regarding the importance of the North American Free Trade Agreement (NAFTA) on behalf of the Greater San Diego Chamber of Commerce. Throughout my 17-year tenure in Congress, I have continued to support free trade and open markets.

NAFTA has been incredibly important to the United States, especially to California, and particularly to Southern California and my district. According to a 2017 report from the Congressional Research Service, NAFTA has increased trade with Mexico and Canada from $290 billion in 1993 to $1.1 trillion in 2016. Product supply chains have grown, jobs are up, and tariffs are down. 14 million American jobs depend on trade with Mexico and Canada according to the U.S. Chamber of Commerce. Moreover, San Diego exports to Mexico are valued at $5.5 billion per year, making it our largest export market.

Negotiations began in August and are expected to complete in March 2018. It is my hope that this timeframe with allow the U.S. to achieve its main objectives, update and modernize the agreement to better foster American job creation in our 21st century global economy. As such, I wish to raise several issues related to energy in the ongoing negotiations.

Energy is an important aspect of the current NAFTA discussion. Currently, U.S. trade with Canada and Mexico in energy commodities, including electricity, liquid fuels, and natural gas, exceeds $140 billion annually. Last year the U.S. enjoyed an energy trade surplus with Mexico of more than $11 billion. At the time NAFTA was created, our energy domestic production was down and we were a large importer; now the circumstances are in reverse. As the U.S. continues to increase domestic supply, we need to ensure private investments and research into cleaner and more efficient fuels, which may lower costs and have environmental benefits.

When NAFTA was first negotiated, Mexico's energy sector was largely closed to foreign investment. In recent years, however, Mexico has enacted constitutional reforms to open the sector to foreign companies, creating huge potential opportunities for U.S. firms. In order to take full advantage of Mexico's market opening, U.S. companies have expressed the need for certainty that their investments will be protected against potential future government mistreatment. The renegotiation process presents an opportunity to lock in Mexico's energy reforms and to maintain and strengthen NAFTA's investment protections.

I appreciate the efforts being made to collaborate on mutual priorities with our neighbors, and modernize and update the deal to spur further job growth, with economic benefits to Southern California and beyond.

402 West Broadway, Suite 1000
San Diego, CA 92101-3585
p: 619.544.1300
www.sdchamber.org

December 13, 2017

Congressman Darrell Issa
California's Forty-Ninth District
2269 Rayburn House Office Building
Washington, DC 20515

Dear Congressman:

The San Diego Regional Chamber of Commerce is grateful for the opportunity to provide a statement for the record of the House Committee on Foreign Affairs TNT Subcommittee's Hearing on The Future of the North American Free Trade Agreement.

The San Diego Regional Chamber of Commerce supports efforts to negotiate much needed updates to NAFTA. We urge the Administration and Congress to avoid tactics that would damage a partnership that has created so much opportunity for our region and the U.S. economy. The integration of the NAFTA partners Mexico and Canada into U.S. supply chains is significant. In my state of California, Mexico is our leading export destination by a long shot. Number two is Canada. In San Diego alone, more than 110,000 jobs are dependent on international trade and together with Baja California businesses in the region have leveraged NAFTA to create a $2.5 billion manufacturing supply chain. We observe a similar phenomenon on the northern border. For example, Michigan's number one export market is Canada, followed by Mexico.

A modernized North American Free Trade Agreement presents increased opportunities for trade with our North American neighbors. However, we are growing increasingly concerned about rhetoric from the administration that would indicate it believes a dismantling of the agreement would be a wise course of action. This course of action would be terribly damaging to the U.S. economy, and would make the administration's stated goal of achieving 3 percent annual economic growth a near impossibility.

A modernized NAFTA will help all of North America remain competitive against other trade blocs, preserving U.S. jobs and discouraging the outflow of capital. The modernized agreement will also ensure that products made in the U.S. can compete on store shelves abroad, while lowering prices and expanding consumer choice here at home.

Furthermore, exiting NAFTA will weaken the trilateral diplomatic relationship North America currently enjoys. In fact, strengthening the relationship was a primary reason NAFTA was created in the first place. We are also concerned that binational collaboration on national security, environmental issues will be weakened, and that siting, designing, and management of future ports of entry may become more difficult.

While we are a staunch supporter of NAFTA, there are many areas for improvement specifically in the areas of improving customs processing with the implementation of the North American Single Window proposal, a three-nation COAC, single company identifier, improved cross-border inter-agency coordination, and unified cargo processing. We also encourage a modernized NAFTA to allow and encourage cross-border investment by the trucking industry to develop a more competitive North American transportation market and a modernized North American Development Bank expanding the Bank's ability to participate in trade facilitation projects at our international land crossings while supporting border security.

Once again, we appreciate the opportunity to provide these comments on NAFTA. Please count on our organization's expertise and experience in cross-border commerce as a resource as you and your colleagues consider the future of the agreement.

Sincerely,

Jerry Sanders
President and CEO

Paola Ávila
Vice President, International Business Affairs
Chair, Border Trade Alliance

9 781984 290922